52 WAYS TO SELL MORE BOOKS!

More books by
Penny C. Sansevieri

NONFICTION

Fans, Followers, and Friends
(Release date: 2012)

Get Published Today!
(Wheatmark, 2011)

Red Hot Internet Publicity
(Cosimo Books, 2009)

Red Hot Internet Publicity
(Morgan James Publishing 2007)

From Book to Bestseller
(Morgan James Publishing, 2007)

Get Published Today
(Morgan James Publishing, 2007)

From Book to Bestseller
(PublishingGold.com, Inc., 2005)

No More Rejections: Get Published Today!
(Infinity Publishing, 2002, 2003)

Get Published! An Author's Guide to the Online Publishing Revolution
(1st Books, 2001)

FICTION

Candlewood Lake
(iUniverse, 2005)

The Cliffhanger
(iUniverse, 2000)

52 WAYS TO SELL MORE BOOKS!

by
Penny C. Sansevieri

52 Ways to Sell More Books!

Copyright © 2012 by Penny C. Sansevieri

All rights reserved. No part of this book shall be reproduced or transmitted in any form or by any means, electronic, mechanical, magnetic, or photographic, including photocopying, recording, or by any information storage or retrieval system or otherwise without prior written permission of the publisher. No warranty liability whatsoever is assumed with respect to the use of the information contained herein. Although every precaution has been taken in the preparation of this book, the publisher and author assume no responsibility for errors or omissions. Neither is any liability assumed for damages resulting from the use of the information contained herein. If you do not wish to be bound by the terms of this paragraph, promptly return this book for a complete refund.

For more information, contact info@amarketingexpert.com

Published by Wheatmark®
1760 E. River Road, Suite 145,
Tucson, Arizona 85718 U.S.A.
www.wheatmark.com

ISBN: 978-1-60494-718-2
LCCN: 2011940946

We'd love your feedback!

Here's how to contact us:

Author Marketing Experts, Inc.
P.O. Box 421156
San Diego, CA 92142
www.amarketingexpert.com

To subscribe to our free newsletter, send an e-mail to
subscribe@amarketingexpert.com

CONTENTS

1. Creating a Marketing Roadmap 1
2. 7 Secrets of Writing a Book That Sells 13
3. Read Blogs in Your Market 15
4. Craft an Exceptional Elevator Pitch 17
5. 5 Steps to Squidoo Success 19
6. How's Your Online Reputation? 23
7. How to Double Your Book Sales on Your Website 24
8. Want to Sell More Books? Go Back to the Basics 27
9. 8 Secrets for Getting into Bookstores 29
10. Maximizing Media Leads 33
11. Sales Advice for New Publishers 36
12. Your 10 Point Website Check Up 43
13. 5 Quick Ways to Rev Up Your Site's Searchability 46
14. 10 Secrets for Savvy Search Engine Optimization 48
15. 12 Secrets to Selling More Books at Events 50
16. How to Monetize "Free" 54
17. Affiliate Marketing 58
18. The Blog Factor 60
19. 10 Reasons Why You Should Be Blogging 63
20. The Real Secret to Twitter 65
21. How to Look Good Online 68

22. 12 Things Authors Do to Sabotage Their Success 70
23. Never Sell Your Book 74
24. The Power of Social Networks 76
25. 14 Ways to Make Your Facebook Page Fun & Lively 80
26. 10 Secrets of a Super Blogger 83
27. Social Networking on Blogs 86
28. What the Shopping Channels Can Teach Us About Selling 89
29. The Book Signing Checklist 92
30. Creating Powerful Content That Will Help You Sell Books 96
31. Networking 99
32. 5 Fun Things You Can Do with Video! 101
33. One Minute Marketing 103
34. Everything Is Your Resume 105
35. 50 Things Under 50 Bucks to Promote Your Book 108
36. The Importance of Consistency 112
37. 12 Ways to Create a Mailing List That Will Sell Books 113
38. 30 Ways to Make Yourself Irresistible to the Media 117
39. 4 Tips on What NOT to Say (or Pitch or Do) to
    Get Your Book Reviewed 122
40. The Quickest Way to Kill Your Online Success 124
41. 5 Steps for Crafting the Perfect Book Review Pitch 127
42. Your Rockin' Red Hot Media Room 131
43. Beyond the Bookstore 134
44. 7 Secrets to Getting into Libraries 138
45. 20 Ways to Drive More Traffic to Your Website and Blog 141
46. 50 Things to Tweet About 146
47. Host a Video Contest 150
48. The Power and SEO Behind Blog Commenting 151
49. 6 Simple Ways to Promote Your YouTube Channel 154
50. Getting a Head Start on Holiday Sales 157

51. 6 Things Your Website Should Tell Book Reviewers About You (and Your Book) 159
52. 10 Things Your Friends Can Do to Help You Sell More Books 162

Bonus Tip! Why (Some) Authors Fail 164

About Penny C. Sansevieri & Author Marketing Experts, Inc. 170

52 WAYS TO SELL MORE BOOKS!

STRATEGY 1
CREATING A MARKETING ROADMAP

After you've gone through the timing of how and what you'll be doing, it's important to decide which marketing options are right for you. The plan for your marketing is like a roadmap. You'd never consider driving from San Diego to New York without a map, nor should you embark on a marketing program without some kind of a map to guide you through the process.

The following will help you start to formulate your marketing roadmap. Keeping in mind that this plan should be flexible and may fluctuate depending on changes dictated by the market, seasons, or current affairs.

Comparative Titles

So who else has written on your topic and what have they written about? It's always a good idea to know your competition. Use this table as a guideline for information gathering. Having this title information could really help you in your research, market analysis, and/or pitching for other experts to blurb your book! Use the chart below and try to find at least five or six other similar titles.

TITLE	PUBLISHER	WHEN RELEASED	PAGES	LIST PRICE	STILL IN PRINT?

Now you'll want to list the ways in which your book is unique compared to these titles.

There's no reason why you can't write on a similar topic as long as your topic is different or an updated version of information that's already been published. Use the following format to help formulate a title comparative and dig into the reasons why and how your book will differentiate itself from books that are already out there. You'll want to do this for each title you're comparing for buying this book. Keep in mind that anything you create here might be used in your marketing or sales copy!

Title: _____

My book is different because:

1. _____

2. _____

3. _____

4. _____

5. _____

Who Will Buy Your Book?

We talked earlier about knowing who your reader is, but now I'd like you to dig a little deeper into the psyche and buying habits of the person who will purchase your book. Ideally you should have one main market and several sub-markets. For example, you might have a book geared toward busy moms; mothers would then be your primary target, a sub-target of that might be grandparents (buying copies for their busy daughters) or single dads looking for a little parenting wisdom. Let's take a look at your primary target first. Ask yourself, who is your reader?

My reader is: _____ Female _____ Male

Age range: _____ to _____

Religion: _____ or ☐ Doesn't matter

Groups and/or associations my reader belongs to:

1. _____

2. _____

3. _____

4. _____

5. _____

Does your reader go to any conferences or trade shows? These could be great places to market your book. Do a quick Internet search to see if you can find conferences and events. Then keep these in a file so you can pitch to them once the book comes out. For each conference listing I'll want you to list how you could participate in this event. You'll note that "get a booth in the trade show" is near the bottom. There's a reason for this. Depending on the cost of the booth and your exposure at the trade show it doesn't always make sense to display your book. Often the cost of the booth is too high to warrant this. Consider doing a speaking engagement instead or better yet, do a speaking engagement then see if you can share a booth with several other authors! That way you're sharing the expense of the booth, getting help to man it for the entire show and giving yourself a place to meet with interested buyers after your talk!

1. _____

    Here's how I can participate:

    ☐ Potential speaking engagement

    ☐ Hot networking opportunity

    ☐ Get a booth in the trade show

    ☐ Great event, but it's information gathering only

2. _____

    Here's how I can participate:

    ☐ Potential speaking engagement

    ☐ Hot networking opportunity

    ☐ Get a booth in the trade show

☐ Great event, but it's information gathering only

3. _____

   Here's how I can participate:

   ☐ Potential speaking engagement

   ☐ Hot networking opportunity

   ☐ Get a booth in the trade show

   ☐ Great event, but it's information gathering only

4. _____

   Here's how I can participate:

   ☐ Potential speaking engagement

   ☐ Hot networking opportunity

   ☐ Get a booth in the trade show

   ☐ Great event, but it's information gathering only

5. _____

   Here's how I can participate:

   ☐ Potential speaking engagement

   ☐ Hot networking opportunity

   ☐ Get a booth in the trade show

   ☐ Great event, but it's information gathering only

Targeting a city or region

Does your book have a strong demographic interest? For example, is it set in a particular town or does it have a cluster of readers in one region compared to another? Consider this before you launch into your marketing campaign. I've had book that I've marketed in one region and one region only because of its significance to the area. If your book falls into this category you might want to figure this out early on and do a laser focused target on that region rather than diluting your efforts on a nationwide campaign.

Regional areas that are significant to this book and why:

1. _____

   This region is significant because: _____
   _____

2. _____

   This region is significant because: _____
   _____

3. _____

   This region is significant because: _____
   _____

Emotional Hot Buttons

Emotional hot buttons are important, we all buy on emotion. Whether we desire to be slimmer, wealthier, happier or smarter, a hot button drives all of our purchases. List at least five of your reader's emotional hot buttons:

1. _____
2. _____
3. _____
4. _____
5. _____

Once you've finished your primary reader, you'll want to do this for any subgroups you'll be marketing to as well.

Now you've developed hooks for your book. If all of these factors aren't addressed in your book you might want to include them. Remember the more hot buttons you address, the more reasons your reader will have to buy your book!

Where will your reader buy your book? This is an important question. We all assume that our readers will buy our books in bookstores but given what we've covered in this book, by now you know that the bookstore component might not be as significant as you once thought. Right now, let's brainstorm some other places that your reader might buy your book. Think of: electronics stores, hobby stores, grocery stores, coffee houses, auto dealerships (maybe as a giveaway), clothing stores, etc.

1. _____
2. _____
3. _____
4. _____
5. _____

Do your readers surf the Net? In all likelihood they probably do. Internet promotion is the single biggest way to promote your book so don't overlook the power of the Web. List a few areas of interest you might be able to tie into. Remember that you'll be going after not just your primary reader but all subgroups as well. Once you're done with this, I'm going to ask you to research a few sites so don't worry about listing them here, all we want to do is look at the specific groups you're going to target.

My readers surf the following interest groups:

1. _____
2. _____
3. _____
4. _____
5. _____

Some websites that might be of interest:

www. _____

www. _____

www. _____

www. _____

www. _____

www. _____

www. _____

www. _____

www. _____

www. _____

Genres and Subgenres

Getting to know your genre is very important. Take a look at your primary genre and all subgenres. Keep in mind that while you might have multiple groups of readers, you might only have one genre and that's ok. Your book *must* fit into one primary genre. You can genre-straddle as I call it. If your book does not fit into a main genre then you're going to have to rewrite it until it does. I'm very serious about this, more books have failed because they're "fuzzy" on their genres. Be lightning specific otherwise rewrite until you are!

Main genre: _____

Secondary genre: _____

It's a good idea to get to know your genre, just like you got to know your reader. Do a quick search on Google for news items in your genre-topic and see what you can pull up. Also, ask your local bookstore what they know about your genre and how well it might be selling. This is a good test for the future marketability of your book so don't overlook it!

Significant Dates or Holidays

When you're planning your campaign, it's easy to get caught up in the moment and just start marketing and while that may be a good thing, there might be positioning factors you're overlooking. Calendar dates, seasons and holidays are all things you can use as "hooks" to promote your book.

Seasons

The following season(s) is significant to my book and here's why:

Season: _____

Significance: _____

Holidays and Calendar Hooks

Remember, especially when it comes to holidays and calendar hooks, the more the merrier so get really creative with this. Think outside the book when it comes to these tie-ins. We all know about Valentine's Day, Christmas and Halloween but how about the following you might not have considered:

January 1: Customer Service Day

January 12: Clean Off Your Desk Day

January is Financial Wellness Month

While not "holidays" per se they are calendar hooks just the same. So start by doing an Internet search on your topic and then try finding not only holidays but also calendar hooks you might be able to use to promote your book!

If you're at a loss for ideas, here are a few I have used that worked very well for our authors:

Holiday: Valentine's Day

Hook: Did you know you could meet Mr. Right in a soup kitchen?

The story behind the hook: Our volunteerism author commented on how singletons are meeting their significant others while volunteering. While her book did not focus on singles and volunteerism, she knew enough about this topic to comment on it. Once we did our research we found that single volunteer organizations were springing up all across the country.

Holiday: Christmas

Hook: Give your kids the gift of laughter this holiday season!

The story behind the hook: We were working with an author who specialized in the importance of using humor with children. He offered ways to give kids the gift of a lifetime: laughter.

Calendar hook: Fire Prevention Week

Hook: How to Get Organized Without Resorting to Arson

The story behind the hook: Our author had a book about organization but the title pulled right into Fire Prevention Week, so while promoting it around other dates that supported organization, we also pushed it during Fire Prevention Week!

The following holiday(s) is significant to my book and here's why:

Holiday: _____

It's significant because: _____

Holiday: _____

It's significant because: _____

Holiday: _____

It's significant because: _____

Calendar hooks:

Calendar hook: _____

It's significant because: _____

Calendar hook: _____

It's significant because: _____

Calendar hook: _____

It's significant because: _____

Budget

Have a look back through our budgeting suggestions and create a budget that you feel you can live with and is sufficient to support your book. Here are a few of the major categories you might want to consider. Keep in mind that since every marketing plan is different, cost components will vary; don't forget to add the ones that are right for your project!

Marketing Budget: _____

Book Purchases: _____

Postage: _____

Postcards/bookmarks: _____

Website: _____

Travel: _____

Book Reviews

Industry book reviewers. If you're submitting to industry book reviewers like Library Journal you'll want to list them here (for a list of reviewers, see our book: From Book to Bestseller). You'll no doubt want to list more than five of them but this will at least give you a good start!

1. _____
2. _____
3. _____
4. _____
5. _____

Print media reviewers. Which newspapers or magazines will you submit to? List a few of them here that you think would be an appropriate target for you:

1. _____
2. _____
3. _____
4. _____
5. _____

Regional reviewers. Who is in your own backyard that you've overlooked? Consider targeting local newspapers and publications. Regional media is always interested in local authors!

1. _____
2. _____
3. _____
4. _____
5. _____

Trade reviewers. Does your industry have any trade magazines like CEO journals, medical journals, military magazines, etc.? Don't overlook this vital step. What better place to get a review than in a publication that's 100% your readership!

1. _____
2. _____
3. _____
4. _____
5. _____

Book Events

Now that you've done all of this information gathering, I would bet that you're thinking of a bunch of other places to do book signings other than a bookstore. Why not brainstorm for a bit and list them here!

"I'm thinking outside the bookstore box! Here's where I plan to do events for my book."

1. _____
2. _____
3. _____
4. _____
5. _____

Media

And what marketing roadmap would be complete without addressing the media you might be targeting? But be cautious here. When it comes to media it's easy to subscribe to a spray and pray theory. Much like you broke down book reviews, I want you to get very clear on the type of media your reader reads, watches or listens to. That is the only media you should be targeting. You should have your list of publications that your reader reads already taken care of under book reviews so we'll just focus on broadcast for this exercise.

List five TV shows and five radio shows you know you'll want to target. Yes, you can do a lot more but for the purposes of getting this portion of your marketing plan complete, I'll limit you to five. Feel free to use an extra sheet if inspiration strikes!

TV Show _____

TV Show _____

TV Show _____

TV Show _____

TV Show _____

Radio Show _____

Radio Show _____

Radio Show _____

Radio Show _____

Radio Show _____

7 SECRETS OF WRITING A BOOK THAT SELLS

It's one thing to write a book, it's an entirely different thing to write one that's a saleable, viable, marketable product. Ensuring the success of a book is something even the biggest publishers have never been able to guarantee. Mitigating circumstances, flash trends and world events will all affect buyer preferences. That said, there are still ways to leverage the sales-factor in your favor and here's how you do it.

1. **Know your readers.** We're not just talking about whether your readers are male or female. You'll want to know myriad factors about your audience. How old are your readers (age range)? Are readers married, single, or divorced? Where do your readers reader live (generally)? What do your readers do for a living? What other books/publications do they read? Develop a profile that includes where they shop, what clubs do they belong to, etc. These elements will help you incorporate these aspects into your book *and* help you unearth salient marketing opportunities (i.e., publications and stores).

2. **Know your market.** What's the market like for your book? Is there a trend out there you're positioning yourself towards? Are you reading all the publications related to this topic/trend? Are there any "holes" out there your book could fill? What's the future for this market/topic? For example, let's say you're a fiction writer looking to publish chick lit. Go to any bookstore and you can't help but spot the cutsie, pink, cartoonish covers. Many thought this trend was dying out, but it has recently seen another surge. What do you know about trends related to your book/topic/audience?

3. **Similar books.** What else has been published on your topic? Have you read all 10 books in your category? If you haven't, you should. You'll want to know everything you can about what's out there and how it's being perceived in the marketplace. It's never a problem having a similar topic. When I published No More Rejections—Get Published Today, I knew there were other books out there on marketing. I read them all-then angled my book differently.

4. **Getting and staying current.** What's going on in your industry today? What are some hot buttons? What are people looking for? What's next on the horizon for this topic/audience? If you can't seem to gather this information through traditional channels, why not survey your target audience? There are a number of places to run free surveys, Survey Monkey is one of them: http://www.surveymonkey.com.

5. **Follow the media.** What's the media talking about these days? Keep track of media buzz--what they're paying attention to and what they're writing about. Delve beyond the front page of your paper to the second or third page and see what's filling the pages. If you can get your hands on out-of-state papers, do a comparative review. Do you see a trend in coverage? Is there something that seems to be getting more buzz even if it's on page six?

6. **Talk, teach and listen.** One of the best ways I've found to get in touch with my audience was to teach a class and do speaking engagements. When I was putting together my book, Get Published Today, I found that the classes I taught provided valuable information for creating a great book because they put me directly in touch with my audience!

7. **Timing is everything.** When do you plan to release your tome? Are you releasing around a holiday or anniversary? Could you take advantage of any upcoming event and/or holiday for your book launch?

STRATEGY 3
READ BLOGS IN YOUR MARKET

It's really that simple: read what others are saying about your market. Even if you write fiction you can read up on publishing and other topics related to your book.

And why would you want to do this? Here are 5 reasons why you should stay dialed into your market online:

1. You'll hear about trends faster if you keep reading blogs by thought leaders in your market. Generally if an idea is good, you'll see it on a few blogs before it hits the news.

2. It's a great way to connect with others. I talk about this in Social Networking on Blogs (Strategy #27).

3. You won't be clueless. Let's face it, the worst thing that could happen is that you get a media interview and the interviewer asks you a question you should know the answer to, but you don't. We can't be expected to know everything but you should keep tabs on your market.

4. Great ideas for blogging. If you're eager to find new blog topics, why not dig into trending topics? The more blogs you read, the more ideas you'll get.

5. Sales ideas. Not only will you stay dialed into your market but reading blogs in your industry might give you new sales ideas or new ways to market your book.

So what's the best way to read blogs? Subscribe to the RSS feed (really simple syndication) and capture all your blog listings in one spot like a Google-i page, which is a page that you customize via Google. I run all my feeds though there and it's in one place. Easy!

How Popular is Your Topic?

One way to find out is to track it on Google Alerts. Try plugging in your keyword to see what comes up. You can access Google Alerts by going to Google and typing in Google Alerts in the search bar. Alerts are free and a really easy way to track what's happening in your market. Keeping track of what's being said, featured and written about your brand is a good way to know how popular it is and who is saying what in your market.

STRATEGY 4: CRAFT AN EXCEPTIONAL ELEVATOR PITCH

What is an elevator pitch and why do you need one? An elevator pitch is a short one to two sentence description about the book. It's the briefest of the brief descriptions you can come up with. The reason elevator pitches are important is that we have an ever shrinking attention span, and so you need to capture someone's attention in a very short, succinct pitch.

How do you begin crafting an elevator pitch? Well, the first thing is to look at the core of your book. What is your book about, really? Looking at the core of your book will help you determine the primary message. The next piece of this is to look at the real benefits to the reader. Not what you think the reader wants but what they actually need: What's in it for the reader?

When I worked with people on elevator pitches I found that they often keep the best sentence for last. This comes from being an author and saving the crescendo of the story until the final chapter. You don't want to do that in an elevator pitch. You want to lead with the tease that will pull the reader in.

When would you use an elevator pitch? You might use it to promote yourself to the media, or to book a speaking event, or to pitch a blogger. Elevator pitches can be used for a variety of reasons and in a variety of ways. Once you create a great elevator pitch you may find yourself using it over and over again. That's a good thing!

Components of a great elevator pitch

All elevator pitches have particular relevance to them, but for the most part every elevator pitch has at least one or more of the following:

- Have emotional appeal
- Be insightful
- Matter to your reader!
- Be helpful
- Be timely

Essential Elements of a Powerful Elevator Pitch

1. **Concise.** Your page needs to be short, sweet and to the point.
2. **Clear.** Save your five-dollar words for another time. For your elevator pitch to be effective, you must use simple language any layperson could understand. If you make someone think about a word, you'll lose him or her and the effectiveness of your elevator pitch will go right out the window as well.
3. **Passion.** If you're not passionate about your topic, how do you expect anyone else to be?
4. **Visual.** Use words that bring visual elements to your reader's mind. It will help to make your message more memorable, as well as bring the reader into your story.
5. **Stories.** And speaking of stories, people love stories. So the one, and perhaps the biggest element of the elevator pitches: tell the story. I also find that when the pitch is woven into the story it often helps to create a smoother presentation.

How to Craft Your Killer Elevator Pitch

- **Write it down.** Start by telling a very short story in two paragraphs. This will get the juices flowing. As you start to edit your story down from let's say 200,000 words to two paragraphs you'll start to see why it's important to pull only the most essential elements from your story to craft your elevator pitch.

- **Make a list.** Make a list of 10 to 20 things that your book does for the reader. These can be action statements, benefits or book objectives.

- **Record yourself.** Next, you're going to want to get a recorder to record yourself. See how you sound, I can almost guarantee that you will not like the first few drafts that you do. That is actually a really good thing because if you like the first thing that you write, it probably won't be that effective. Recording yourself will help you listen to what you're saying and figure out how to fine-tune it.

- **Rest.** I highly recommend that you give yourself enough time to do your elevator pitch. Ideally you want to let it rest overnight, if not longer. Remember, the elevator pitch is perhaps the most important thing that you created in your marketing package. You want to make sure it's right.

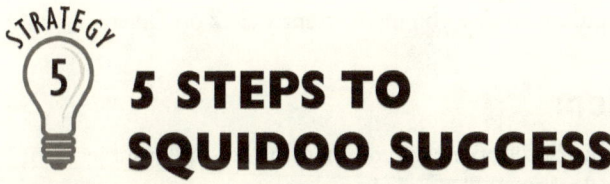

5 STEPS TO SQUIDOO SUCCESS

Squidoo is a great way to promote yourself and your book; once you have built a Squidoo Lens you can work on promoting it both within Squidoo and the search engines (like Google).

But let's take a look at how to get from point A—creating your lens, to point B—promoting it...

Basic Squidoo Instructions:

Choose your lens title for branding purposes that are in line with the goals of your book or your writing career. Do you have multiple books planned? Perhaps the lens should use your name. Are you interested in strongly promoting one of your titles or an issue? The lens should then reflect that.

Create your lens using original content and graphics because those are important to the search engines. To move forward from here, you'll want to get some traffic to your lens, which you can do when you visit other lenses in your area/topic on Squidoo and post comments that invite those individuals to visit your lens. This will help you gain ranking and recognition on Squidoo and should be ongoing.

Here's How:

When you log in to Squidoo you can click on My Dashboard and follow the tabs across the top to edit information, like that in your Profile.

Under the Lens Title in your Dashboard, you can click on the options to View, Edit, Delete and Stats along with some additional information like your overall rank in Squidoo, and the last date your lens was updated. **Don't hit delete, ever–you don't want to lose your lens!**

When you click on the Edit link, you'll see that Squidoo lenses are created with different sections or what they call modules. You can edit an existing module and you can add modules. If you scroll down and look to the right, you'll see an area that says "Export this lens." This serves as your backup and you should do this regularly in case you inadvertently click on Delete.

Lens Promotion:

Cross-promotion within Squidoo means commenting on similar subject lenses and getting backlinks to your lens, and in some cases getting your book added to their lens. Typically after you visit another lens they will visit your lens and leave a comment in turn. Not only do you gain exposure on Squidoo, you can make some valuable contacts.

You can also join Squidoo groups in your areas of interest to continue making contacts and promoting yourself on the site. For instance, if your topic is eco-friendly wellness, look up green living, health and fitness—you'll find plenty of groups to join. Adding your lens to a group will create several more links to your lens from within Squidoo, and will help your lens get found from more places. In the sidebar of your lens will be a little link list (under the heading Explore More) with links to all of the groups that your lens is a member of. This helps your Google ranking if you are joining relevant groups. Joining relevant groups helps your lens because any visitors to the group (or to a member lens) can find other lenses on the same topic. Because you're grouped with like interests, it's that much easier for people to find you.

You can also set up your lens to send a Tweet to Twitter any time you update your Squidoo page—and this will help you with generating new content for Twitter.

Things You Can Continue to Do:

- Always save the modules you edit and republish the lens after every update.
- Every couple of weeks add or change content in a Text module (even a sentence makes a difference). A small change will work to keep you on the radar of Squidoo and Google.
- Lensroll it on your other lenses. If you don't have additional lenses yet, you can lensroll favorite and relevant lenses by other lensmasters. On your lens, you'll see down the side of the page, the word "Lensroll." If you click it, you'll be taken to a page where you can choose one of your other lenses

from the list and clicking to confirm will create a 'lensroll' link to your new lens from your old one. The link will be featured in the sidebar either under the heading "More Great Lenses" or "Lensroll." Use this to showcase your related lenses to your visitors. It helps your lensrank too!

- Email your list (if you have one) and ask them to visit your lens, rate it, sign the guestbook, and bookmark it in return for some sort of freebie, like a 5-page report, or whatever else is relevant to your book or your list.
- Start being an important part of the Squidoo community. Visit other lenses with the same topic and sign their guestbook, rate their lens, and ask them to come visit your lens, too. Be yourself, don't spam other lenses with gratuitous promotions, you wouldn't want them to do it to you!

Moving Forward:

You will find tons of helpful information at: http://www.squidoo.com/theanswerdeck/hq.

There are two free ebooks there to help you master lens crafting. These two free ebooks were written by the Squidoo staff, including its founder Seth Godin.

The first ebook is called Calamari: the Official Squidoo How-To. It walks you through lens making from conception to publication and beyond. The second ebook is called The Joy of Squidoo: the Official Recipe Guide. This ebook deals more with what your target audience is looking for.

Another thing that you can do to increase traffic after each new change is to go to: http://pingomatic.com/ and fill out the first three lines, click on Check Common and then Send Pings. This alerts the Google spiders that a change has been made instead of waiting for them to find you. You don't have to create an account—it's very simple!

Update your lens regularly with small snippets of information or articles. Social networking is about having conversations with people who are interested in the same subjects as you. Find existing conversations (lenses) and add value (by commenting on their lens). You'll find Squidoo is a great way to continue building your brand!

How Much Power Does Your Headline Pack?

Advanced Marketing Institute has a free Emotional Marketing Value Headline Analyzer for analyzing the emotional marketing value of a headline. I use it for finding good fit alternatives for my speeches, blogs, newsletters, and articles. Just type in your headline, and it will give you an "emotional rating" for the title based on your word choice. It takes just a few seconds, and has proven helpful for crafting a good title. http://www.aminstitute.com/headline/

JUST BECAUSE:

Great Places to Donate Books
- Soldiers' Angels < http://soldiersangels.org/index.php?page=books>
- Got Books? <http://www.gotbooks.com/donate_books.php>
- Kids In Distressed Situations (K.I.D.S.) <http://www.kidsdonations.org/index.htm>
- Reader to Reader <http://www.readertoreader.org/donate.html>
- Pages for Children <http://www.pagesforchildren.com/Donations.htm m/Donations.htm> *
- International Book Bank <http://www.internationalbookbank.org/donatebooks.html

Contributed by Paula Krapf, COO Author Marketing Experts, Inc.

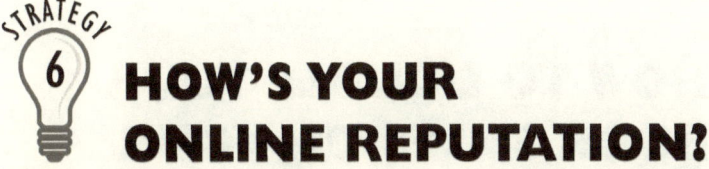

STRATEGY 6
HOW'S YOUR ONLINE REPUTATION?

For years Google Alerts has been great for watching what's being said about you online. But now there are a few other players, so you should check out these online reputation management tools. They're a great way to keep track of what's being said about you, your book and/or product online:

Addict-o-matic: I was really surprised when I first logged on to discover how much stuff was out there on me that Google Alerts didn't pick up. This is a free service and a great resource, the only complaint I have is there's no RSS feed that I can subscribe to to keep me posted on weekly or even daily additions. Hopefully that will come soon, for now, here's the link: http://addictomatic.com/. The best part about this service is that it doesn't require that I sign in or sign up for anything. I like that. I have way too many subscriptions and passwords I can't remember as it is.

Filtevox.com: I liked it but I had to sign up which I didn't like. So many services, so little time. Also very thorough and free for the basic service.

Trackur.com: This site claims to be Google alerts on steroids. The write-ups I've seen are great and the site or the write-ups don't lie. It's not a free service (though they offer a free trial) but the service is quite thorough and outstanding. Give it a shot and see what you think.

STRATEGY 7
HOW TO DOUBLE YOUR BOOK SALES ON YOUR WEBSITE

Face it, times are tough! The economy blah, blah, blah. Tell me something new. The key is: Everyone loves a bargain, especially today. And bargains drive sales.

Here's a great way you can explode your sales:

Call a bargain what you want: a discount, coupon, sale, bonus package, gift with purchase, etc. The point is, people love it. At one point we tried an experiment. We decided to bundle my latest title: *Red Hot Internet Publicity*, with an older book called *Book Promotion Made Easy*. By older I don't mean outdated, I mean that it was an evergreen title, older to the list so the author had moved on from aggressively promoting it. The match was perfect and on the first launch our sales of *Red Hot Internet Publicity* quadrupled. I was stunned.

For many publishers, a backlist is either gold or stagnant. In either case, there's likely a title that you can pair up with a newer one you are promoting. In the case of the bundle mentioned above, I didn't even write *Book Promotion Made Easy*. So if you're looking for pairing options and you don't have a suitable book in-house to pair it with, consider co-promoting the titles with another author. Not only will you get a quality bundle, but if they have a list they can promote it to you can participate in their promotion as well. It's a win-win.

The breakdown was easy:
- We bundled together my new book *Red Hot Internet Publicity* with Book Promotion Made Easy. Total value: $30.95.
- Red Hot is $18.95 and Book Promotion Made Easy is $12.00.

- Book Marketing Experts offered the bundle for $20. That's a 35% savings or $10.95.

Want to know how we did it? I'll tell you how you can create your own special website promotions to double or triple sales from your site:

1. Analyze your book and its cost.

2. Look to raise the price of the bundle "a bit" to cover the cost of the add-on or bonus item. No matter what, offer great value to your customer.

3. Look for bonuses you can add in. Successful examples include a booklet, book, ebook, checklist, article, special report, an MP3 audio program or CD.

The key to success is to offer a bonus or package that is valuable to your customers.

That value drives sales.

- If you're going to partner with someone to do this (and what a great idea!) then contact the author/seller. Most vendors, inside and outside publishing, love to make bulk sales at a steep discount. Often 70–80% off retail.
- Don't want to spend money or pair up? No worries. As an author or publisher you can write your own special report, booklet, ebook, etc. Just make sure it has a significant value.
- Assign a value to your new publication. Some ebooks have a price of $9.97, $17.00, $17.95, $19.95, $24.50 and in some cases even higher. Set the price based on your market's perceived value of the product.
- Round up the price. Make it easy to make a purchase and make the dollars and cents clear.
- We rounded up the price of **Red Hot Internet Publicity** from $18.95 to $20 and gave away Book Promotion Made Easy for $0.00.
- It's important, however to explain the savings clearly so the customer sees the great value you're offering.
- Add a special landing page to your website that promotes your special offer.
- For an example, here's ours: http://www.amarketingexpert.com/diy-store/books-books-books/two-books-for-20/

- Link the landing page (offer) to your shopping cart, PayPal, etc.
- Fill the orders asap. Buyers are a very impatient group these days.
- Promote your package to your mailing list and if you're partnering with someone, make sure they promote it to their list as well.

Book bundling is a fun and easy way to increase sales of virtually any book. I have found that when I pair up Book Promotion Made Easy with my book at speaking events, I quadruple the sales there as well. Two books for $20? You bet that's a great offer and not only that, it moves books and moves them quickly.

The key is to feed into the bargain mentality that seems to permeate society. You can play the bargain game and win. And the best part? As you're selling all these books you're also growing your mailing list, yes? You better be. As a bonus, we offered a free Twitter class to everyone who bought the bundle. We didn't advertise it though, we told them after their purchase. It adds that special "thank you" to our message and builds customer loyalty. You can come up with something that's included in your confirmation email.

STRATEGY 8
WANT TO SELL MORE BOOKS? GO BACK TO THE BASICS

No matter how much technology changes, no matter what new gizmo is created, there is nothing, I repeat nothing that works better than good, old-fashioned people skills. If you want to sell more books, you need to focus on building relationships. That's not what people want to hear. They want one-button solutions where they can make a million bucks overnight. I don't doubt that somewhere out there, something like that is on the horizon, but not for lasting success. If you want lasting success you need to go back to the basics:

1. Integrity

2. Friendships

3. Great product

Let's begin with the first step, Integrity. That means point blank, doing what you say you're going to do. That means being honest. That means not being so desperate to sell a book or to be famous that you'll tell your potential customer whatever they want to hear to sell a book. It's not worth it and bad news spreads faster than a California wildfire, so don't even try it.

A funny thing happens when you stop pushing your book in front of people, when you take an interest in them instead of talking about yourself. Naturally, they ask you about you. And when they hear that you're an author, oh, my! Then half the work has been done for you. Being an author still has a cachet to it because 90% of Americans have thought about writing a book. There's no need to push. My tip for you is to take an interest in them. Repurpose your campaign to focus on step number 2) Friendships. Build relationships with people because as the old saying goes, "It's hard to say 'no' to people you know."

Your campaign for the first phase should be about identifying which people would appreciate your book the most and then, second, building relationships with them. Maybe they're Mommy bloggers, maybe they're librarians or bookstore owners or message board forum directors, maybe they're teachers or church leaders or maybe they're book club leaders or book reviewers. Work on building friendships with them. In a word, giving. Not taking.

You see, as artists, often our focus is on ourselves. We just spent half a decade slaving over the computer to pump out this thing and we want the world to know about it. But the truth is, no one cares about anything but themselves. It's terrible to say but it's true, and armed with that knowledge, think about what you can do to help people feel good. What can you do to give, to do a favor for someone, to find out what they really care about. Build relationships with people because sooner or later, they'll naturally ask what they can do for you.

And what do you need from them? To promote your step 3) Great product. You see no matter how famous you are, at the end of the day, you need great product. Sure, if Stephen King wrote something on toilet paper, anyone would buy it but word would spread fast if it was literally crap. Even he has to deliver. I find many of the authors I work with are in such a hurry to land an agent that they don't spend as much time honing their craft to perfection. Make a truly dynamic product that more than your mother will love, something that will make us talk about it around the water cooler, and you're already in the top 2% of authors out there.

Focus on these three steps and guaranteed, you'll sell a heck of a lot more books than you normally would.

By Jeff Rivera—Author and Founder of "LandanAgentin7Days.com"

STRATEGY 9
8 SECRETS FOR GETTING INTO BOOKSTORES

Let's face it, regardless of the odds we authors still want to get into bookstores. But if you've been having a hard time with this, take heart. It's getting harder and harder to get into stores, but not impossible. We're going to look at some of the possibilities here.

First, it's important to understand the pressure stores are under right now. With the increased focus on publishers to get their authors out there, bookstores are being given most of their marching orders by their corporate office. Bookstore shelf space is bought and paid for by the New York publishers, making getting on the shelves or display racks a bit tricky—if not impossible.

So here's a game plan for those of you trying to survive outside of the traditional market.

1. **Get to know your local store.** I know this might sound obvious, but you'd be surprised how many authors don't really know the people in their local store. The thing is, if you know them, they know you. Then, when you're ready to promote your book they might be more open to having you in their store if you have taken the time to get to know them.

2. **Events.** One way to get into a bookstore is by doing an event. Sometimes when you do an event the store may stock the book before and after you've done your program. Start to follow the types of events they do at the store. Get an events calendar or get on their email list. You'll start to see trends emerge. For example, they might have an independent author night you could participate in. Also, be cautious for big releases. If you are trying to capture the attention of a store when they're in the middle of a major book launch, you're likely to be ignored.

   a. Book signings are boring; offer to do an event instead. Events are a draw, book signings aren't unless you're a celebrity. Plan to do a talk, educate, entertain, or enlighten. This will be a more attractive pitch to the bookstore and will draw more people to your talk.

b. Get to know the local authors in your area and then offer to plan events for them. Here's how this works: bookstores are inundated with local authors asking for a time slot, but what if you went to the bookstore manager and said that you'd be willing to coordinate a once a month event featuring all the local authors? The bookstore could just refer all local independently published authors to you, you could coordinate this—and guess what? Not only are you helping the store, but guess who's getting a monthly showcase in their store? You. You can do this with more than one store if you have the time, but keep in mind that with cutbacks often one store manager will oversee a few locations so you might only have to go through one person.

c. If they won't let you coordinate a monthly event, suggest that they have an Independent Author Night if they haven't already started this. If they have an Independent Author Night you should definitely participate, it's a great way to gain exposure, not to mention network with some local people.

3. **Distribution.** Making sure that the bookstore can actually acquire the book is often the first step in getting stocked. Bookstores generally tap into two databases for stocking: Baker & Taylor and Ingram. If you're listed there, bookstores can order the book, though a listing in those databases doesn't usually prompt stocking because these are not distributors, they are wholesalers. There's a big difference. Distributors such as IPG, Perseus, and Midpoint actively push the book into the bookstores, or try to sell copies into the stores during their sales push. Wholesalers don't do this, so if you can get a distributor for your book, great! This could really help your in-store success.

4. **Local marketing.** Don't forget any marketing you do locally, whether it's speaking in venues outside of the bookstores, television, radio, or print. All of this can drive traffic into the bookstores. Market locally and when you do, let the stores know you're going to have a feature or appearance so they can stock the book, if they want to. It's always a great idea to get to know the managers or buyers for your local stores so you can alert them to media or an event you're doing. This not only keeps you and your book on their radar screen, but it's a nice courtesy to offer

them. Most managers are stretched pretty thin and appreciate the buying tip, whenever they can get it. Even if they choose not to stock your book the first or second time, keep alerting them to your promotion. Eventually they just might.

5. **Know your Geography.** Let's say you live in New York, but your book is more suited to the Midwest market... Why keep pushing in an area that's already inundated with authors and books and events? Why not push it to a market that's more appropriate for your topic? By doing this you will not only open up channels you might not have considered, but you'll likely do better in sales. When you do this, you should plan to coordinate some marketing around it so folks in that local area are aware that your book is there.

6. **Buy a book.** Don't just wander the store trying to make friends: shop there. Support your local stores regardless of whether they are a chain or independent. You'd be surprised what a difference this makes when you're trying to get to know the folks who could book you for an event or stock the book on their shelves.

7. **Funnel your buyers.** Try as best you can to funnel everyone to one store to purchase your book. If you're having a tough time getting shelf space (and aren't we all?), funneling folks to one store might prompt that store to keep a few copies of your book on hand. Whenever you do local speaking or media, let them know by name and address where they can get your book. Stores have been known to take in books that they're getting lots of requests for, regardless of how they are published. If you're sending people to one store—instead of fragmenting them to a bunch of different ones—you could start building an ongoing interest in reorders, and sometimes all it takes is one store to stock it before the neighboring stores will follow suit.

Getting into bookstores isn't impossible, but it does require a dash of creativity. Keep in mind that if bookstores still aren't receptive after you've tried these tips then maybe you're sitting in a tight market. Areas like Los Angeles, New York and Chicago might be tough areas to get noticed, because these are often the first stops traditional publishers seek when planning author tours and getting stocked on the shelves. If you're near those areas, try looking outside of the city for alternatives that are often overlooked by New York. If that doesn't work for you, then consider non-bookstore shelf space and events. If you're not sure how to do this, check out my other article on events outside of the normal bookstore market: http://huff.to/cx05E2.

Over the years we've planned events for our authors in all sorts of non-bookstore venues such as: video stores, electronics stores, gyms and even grocery stores. If events are your focus, keep an open mind and remember: often the biggest piece of getting your book into a bookstore is the relationship you build with them.

STRATEGY 10: MAXIMIZING MEDIA LEADS

Thanks to HARO (http://www.helpareporter.com/) and similar media leads services, there are media leads out there for everyone, all the time. Media, media, everywhere! The key, however, is to maximize these leads. Often, we think that as long as we respond to them, and give them our information, the hard part is done. That couldn't be farther from the truth. In fact it's really just the beginning. How can you get better exposure for your pitches? Here is a quick guide to pitching these media leads services that will provide you with insight and guidance for better placement and better stickiness to the stories you pitch.

Pitching the right lead: First and foremost, you need to define the right lead to pitch. But really, it's more than that. Keep in mind that for a variety of topics such as finance, dieting and parenting you might find a lot of leads but not all of them are appropriate to your topic. Some people think that you shouldn't pitch anything that isn't 100% spot on. If I followed this way of thinking, I wouldn't have gotten myself into a variety of publications, including Entrepreneur Magazine.

So what's the goal? The goal is to go after as many leads as you can within the appropriate market. For example, if you have a diet book that is focused on a soy based program and you see a lead about getting ready for summer, you might think it seems off, but the idea here might be to pitch them your topic: to help people get ready for summer. The same is true for an article on the high divorce rate and you have a book on making divorce a smoother transition. This could be a great opportunity for you to pitch a sidebar idea on creating a gentler transition for families of divorce.

The idea really is that, to the degree it's appropriate, pitch yourself to as many on-point topics as you can. When I do this, however, I will always address the issue of the topic they pitched and then ask if they are interested in perhaps taking a sidebar angle to the piece or offering an extended insight into their topic. You'd be amazed at how often this gets a response.

Response time: Basically, as fast as you can. You should never, ever, ever sit on a lead unless you need to gather additional data before responding. Don't wait. Period. Remember that you aren't the only person seeing that lead, many of these reporters and journalists get hundreds of responses per lead they send and generally, the first who respond get the most attention. Ignore the deadline and send it right away, if you wait until minutes before the deadline you might get buried in the hundreds of other leads that have flooded the recipient's inbox.

Response: Short, sweet, and to the point. While I suggested in the above tip that you take some liberty with some of your leads and responses, I still recommend keeping it on point and short. In fact I'll often highlight some key points, send the response off and indicate that I'm aware they might be sitting with a flooded inbox and if my response has piqued their interest, I am happy send as much additional data as they need. Also, if appropriate, cite or link to any current articles that you've been featured in online so the media person can see the breadth of your knowledge. Oh and one final note, please, please, please spell check your emails. You'd never send a resume to a potential employer with typos in it, right? So it baffles me that anyone would send an email that wasn't spell checked.

The media are your customers: Remember to always treat media like your customer, and like a consumer, they probably have a lot of choices. Serve them as you would a new client. Give them what they need in a timely fashion and don't under-deliver. Ever. Don't embellish, don't alter the facts and be ready to prove every single point you are making in your pitch.

Managing the responses: As you get responses you should be ready to act immediately. If you are pitching yourself to *any* media you should be checking your email regularly—several times a day in fact. Depending on the story you are pushing for, you should really be on top of your email, all the time, so you can be prepared to respond immediately.

Follow up: Unless you've been tapped by the media person to be in the article don't follow up on a lead you sent, ever. Why? Because if they need you they'll let you know; if they don't, a follow-up email is just annoying. Keep in mind that even if the media person doesn't respond, you might still see some activity from them down the road. This happened to me with an INC online piece. They didn't need me for the original story I had responded to but kept my information on file and used it later. Had I followed up a few times this might not have happened if I had gotten labeled as a "pest"—be careful of the impression you make in email!

You've got placement: Great! Congratulations! So, what now? Well now it's time to promote, promote, promote the lead you were just featured in. Post it to Twitter, list it on your blog and Facebook Fan Page and oh, don't forget to thank the media person too!

How to find great leads: There are a number of great resources out there for finding leads. Here are just a few of them!
- Help A Reporter Out: www.helpareporter.com
- Reporter Connection: www.reporterconnection.com
- Blogger Link Up: www.bloggerlinkup.com
- Pitch Rate: http://pitchrate.presskit247.com/index.asp

Media leads are a great way to get yourself in front of media that need your expertise. I have found media lead responding to be a fantastic way to gain media attention for our authors. Get on the media leads bandwagon and start responding. You never know where you could land a story!

SALES ADVICE FOR NEW PUBLISHERS

You have written and slaved over your book for months, you have taken on the arduous process of learning and working as a publisher. Your book is on a truck, on its way to you. So . . . you're done now, right? Wrong.

Many author/publishers make the mistake of thinking that once they have produced a great book, it will "sell itself." It won't. Never does. Books are remarkably little help in selling themselves. A great cover will help tremendously, a good story is a plus . . . but to make the difference between a good book in your garage and a good book on your neighbors' nightstands, you need sales, marketing and publicity. There are a number of different ways to sell, market and publicize your book, but before we go into that, let's develop a working definition of what sales, marketing and publicity are.

Sales is the act of convincing a retailer or a wholesaler to stock and promote your book.

Marketing is the act of advertising, promoting, and announcing your book to a specific industry and consumer base. Marketing includes postcard mailings to librarians, ads in local movie theaters before the main show, newspaper ads in Sunday supplements, front-of-store tables at bookstores, placement ads in catalogs, and other promotional activities. Online marketing is very popular and effective right now. It is not as driven by ads, but by outreach and "impressions" on other Internet users. What online marketing saves in dollars, it makes up for in time commitments.

Publicity, or "public relations," is the act of securing press for an author or book. Never paid for, publicity is what will get you on *Good Morning America* or into your local newspaper's Lifestyle section. A good publicist will work with editors, writers, producers, and booking staff to get your book and your name out to radio listeners, television audiences, newspaper readers, and magazine subscribers. They will help you craft your message and then disseminate it to the press.

The difference between marketing and public relations is this: If, during the six o'clock news, the anchor reads a story about your book—that is PR. If, during the six o'clock news, a commercial about your book airs between newscasts—that is marketing. You need both to convince a bookstore or large retailer to stock your book.

There are a number of different places where books are sold. They are sold to libraries, bookstores, gift stores, corporations, catalogs, Internet retailers, audiences of speaking engagements, schools, and anywhere readers may be found. Publishers sell their books to people the author knows, people who belong to the same organizations as the author, companies that have expressed a need for the book's information, organizations that want to resell the book as a fundraiser, and retailers that believe they will have a big enough demand to warrant the risk of putting the book on their shelves.

Again, sales is the act of getting a store or retail venue to stock your book. Marketing is the act of letting the end user, the reader, know that your book is available and where to find it. Successful books merge both sales and marketing in a manner that results in a reader purchasing your book and taking it home.

The Importance of understanding and crafting your book's positioning statement: To create a truly effective sales and marketing plan, start with the who, what, where, when, why, and how.

- Who will actually shell out the money to buy your book? Outline their age, finances, gender, and circumstances.
- What makes your book worth the consumer's money?
- Where will your readers find your book?
- When will your readers need your book? At what point in their lives will they need your book?
- Why is your book more appealing than others in the same category? (Be brutally honest here. Do you compete on price? Is your information more up to date?)
- How will your potential readers find out about your book?

Your Positioning Statement

Get all this down on paper and look at it. You are now prepared to write your book's positioning statement. When you are ready to present your book to the world (readers, bookstores, publicists, buyers, etc.), the most important tool in your arsenal will be the positioning statement. This statement is 100—200 words that outline for a potential buyer the reasons why your book will be of interest to their clients. These 100—200 words should not outline what your book is about. This statement exists to talk about the potential market for your book and how you, as the publisher, plan to reach that market.

For example, if you have identified your core readership as business executives looking for a new job, your positioning statement could look something like this:

> *Shut Up and Hire Me* is a step-by-step program designed for the busy business executive. Each chapter was written and designed to be read in less than ten minutes. Unlike other career guides on the shelf today, *Shut Up and Hire Me* draws from the wisdom and experience of CEOs from more than thirty Fortune 500 companies. Interviews, combined with proven techniques, are provided to help executives find and land their next position. Author Bill Billiam has hired top New York PR firm, Blown Out of Proportion, and is the author of such previous works as: *Better Dead than Unemployed* and *More Money for Less Work*.

Your Marketing Statement

When you have your positioning statement done, then it is time to write your marketing statement.

The following example would garner the attention of any buyer:

> *Shut Up and Hire Me* has recently received several rave reviews from *Business Week, USA Today* and MSN Careers. This step-by-step program will be publicized in all the top business magazines and advertised in all major market newspapers. Bill Billiam is the host of *Business with Billiam* on Fox 5 NYC from 2:00 to 2:30 M–F and has a commitment from the *Today Show* for a three-minute segment on their morning telecast.

Your Sales Kit

Once you have the entire positioning statement and Marketing statement completed, you are ready to approach the stores. Stores have a person or a team of people whose job is to choose the books that go on their shelves. They are "buyers." Publishers usually have just one chance to convince these buyers to put their books on their shelves and to do that, you must send them a complete sales kit. This includes, but is not limited to, a cover, a complete outline of the book, your positioning and marketing statements, a few sample chapters, and a one-page sheet listing all the book's pertinent information. When selling a book to the bookstores, libraries and chains, remember that the people seeing your book sales kit see hundreds of sales kits a day. They will choose a very small percentage of the books they see. Your kit can make the difference between a purchase order and a politely worded e-mail (We regret to inform you . . .).

Here is a complete checklist of what is recommended for a sales presentation kit for your buyers:
- Color printout of the cover on heavy, glossy paper
- A bound ARC/galley or comb-bound manuscript if the book is finished. Sample chapters printed out if it is not.
- Fully outlined and explained marketing and publicity plan
- One-page title information sheet with:
- ISBN
- Title
- Subtitle
- Author
- Author bio
- Author hometown
- 100-word description of book
- Order contact information
- Book category
- Retail price
- Page count
- Trim size
- Ship date
- Publication date
- Format
- Print run
- Co-op and advertising budget
- Title and ISBN of previous books by author or in the series
- Title and ISBN of books similar to yours

The Buyers' Budgets and Schedules

The world of books and retail runs on dates and deadlines. You may have the best dating book in the history of the world. It may be the one program that will find true love for anyone who reads it. You may have a personal note from Oprah saying that it changed her life. None of that matters if you do not follow the schedules set by the retailers and wholesalers carrying that book to the people.

Buyers require that publishers present their books five to six months before publication. These stores have very tight budgets, and only allow a buyer to purchase as many books as they can afford in a given month. No matter how much buyers may like a book, if they have spent their budget for that month, they cannot buy it. You may ask, "Why can't they just move the book out a month and buy the next month?" Well, they can. But they often won't.

If buyers start "borrowing" from future months, it only takes a few months of playing fast and loose with budgets for the whole system to get muddled up, and they will very likely lose their jobs. They like their jobs. A lot.

To be fair to everyone, a buyer has to buy a book in the month that you, the publisher, declare as the publishing date. You set that date, and you (usually) have to live with it. If your book is not coming together as quickly as you had hoped or if you are late getting the information to the buyer, it would be wise to move the pub date out to the six-month mark. I know you want to see your books published and available as soon as possible, but not following the correct procedure will doom your project to a future on a few local bookstore shelves and being pitched on the Internet. If you want a chance at a real, national release, you have to follow the rules.

Every buyer is required to buy books within a set budget and schedule. Asking a buyer to find money for your book in May when his or her budget is already spent through October will not go well. Work within the system. It shows knowledge of the buyer's predicament and a respect for his or her constraints.

Are there exceptions? All the time. Should you count on being one of those exceptions? No. Exceptions to these schedules and budget timelines are created only when a book gets huge national TV or magazine exposure (*NY Times, People, USA TODAY* ... not your local Fox morning show or the Mensa Bulletin), or when there is sufficient reason to convince buyers to go to their bosses and prove that your book is worth going outside the lines. These buyers see hundreds of new books a day. Do not count on getting their attention long enough to make your case. Just follow the rules, and it will make everyone happy. Once buyers gather all the information on all the books scheduled for a particular month, they will go through and evaluate each on its merits, marketability, and salability. At that point, they choose the books they want and compare their list of books with the amount of money they have budgeted for that month and see if they can buy all the books they liked. They won't be able to. They never have the space or money to buy every book that they think has merit.

Now comes the sad process of skipping books that might have done well because there is another book that they believe will do better. Sometimes, they won't skip the book altogether; they will cut the number of stores that will carry the book down to just the author's hometown to see how it sells there. If they can prove to their bosses that your book has potential by seeing big sales locally, that is often a good way to get them to eventually take in more.

Promotions

If you are focusing your sales efforts on the national chains and wholesalers, you may be asked to participate in a promotional program. Chains charge approximately $1 to $2 a unit to put your book on a table or in a themed display across the country. It is common to spend $3,000 to $3,500 in "co-op funds" to put 2,000 books on a display. Wholesalers have a number of great programs designed to get your book in front of the biggest book buyers and librarians in the country. These programs cost anywhere from $200 for a catalog annotation to several thousands for a full, seasonal program of print, galley, and online outreach.

Creating Your Sales Schedule

Let's take a look at the items you will want to cover in the months leading up to your publication:

Eight months before your book's pub date:
- Send your book's data to the wholesalers, retailers, Internet companies, and industry databases.

Seven months before your book's pub date:
- Contact all database departments and confirm that your book is in their systems.
- Create packages containing sample chapters, a color cover, and a table of contents.

- Hire publicity and marketing firms or create publicity and marketing plans on your own.

Six months before your book's pub date:
- Send sales packets to the wholesale and retail buyers.
- Write cover copy and marketing plan for back of the Advance Reader's Copy.
- Design ARC.
- Send ARC files to printer.
- Send ARCs to buyers.
- Call buyers to follow up and present book information. Request promotion and placement for your book.

Five months before your book's pub date:
- Research potential promotion and placement opportunities appropriate for your book (front-of-store tables, postcard mailings, Internet ads...).
- Check to see that all databases have your book information and have it correctly.

Four months before your book's pub date:
- Send ARCs to reviewers.

Three months before your book's pub date:
- Call reviewers to follow up on review packages.
- Buy ads and initiate marketing for launch during pub month.

Two months before your book's pub date:
- Send finished books to buyers with request for orders and updates on your marketing buys.
- Participate in a library outreach campaign through your distributor or find a service that allows publishers to announce books to librarians.
- Send copies of your finished book to companies, corporations, and catalogs that you feel best represent your book's audience.

One month before your book's pub date:
- Call all key buyers and confirm orders are in place.

Contributed by: Amy Collins, Senior Partner, The Cadence Group www.thecadencegrp.com

YOUR 10 POINT WEBSITE CHECK UP

So you have a website, congratulations! Now let's make sure it's doing what it is supposed to be doing for you. Read: selling your book or product. While websites will differ in color, layout and target audience, there are a few things that need to remain consistent. Let's take a look at them.

1. **Editing.** Your website needs to be edited. There is no discussion on this topic at all. And don't self-edit. Hire someone to go through your site page by page and make sure you don't have any typos. Finding mistakes on your site is like finding typos on a resume. Doesn't bode too well, does it?

2. **Website Statistics.** Do you know your site stats? Did you even know you can get them? Site statistics are part of every website design. If you don't have access to them, make sure you get this information. A good site stat service is Google Analytics, pretty comprehensive actually and easy to integrate into your site. You should know your traffic patterns and learn to read these reports (it's a lot easier than it sounds). This way you'll know what your site is doing and what it isn't.

3. **Media Room.** Even if you have never had any TV or radio appearances, you should have a media room. The media room is a great place to list all of your accomplishments as it relates to the book. Also, it's a good place to put your bio, picture (both of you and the book cover), as well as media Q&A and a host of other items.

4. **Website Copy.** Your website isn't a magazine, people don't read—they scan—so make sure your site isn't so crammed with text that it's not scanable. Ideally your home page should have no more than 200 to 250 words. Also, make sure you have a clear call to action. You want your

visitors to do something on your site, yes? Make sure they know what that is, clearly and precisely.

5. **Store.** Yes, you should have a place for people to buy on your site, even if it means sending them off to Amazon.com or somewhere else to make their purchase. One key factor though: don't make them hunt for it. Shorten the staircase. In other words, make it easy to find your stuff and then give them the quickest route to get there to purchase the item.

6. **Design.** I have two major rules in life, you should never cut your own hair or design your own website. Period. End of story. Why? Because much like editing our own books, we're just too darned close to our message to be able to do it justice. Also, most of us are writers, not designers. Hire someone, invest the money, you'll be glad you did. When you're designing, also remember that your homepage should only do one thing. Your website can sell a lot of things, including any consulting or speaking services you offer, but your home page should be focused in on one major item. Surfers spend on average of 1/50th of a second on a website, if they have to stop and try and figure out what your site is about they will leave. I call it surf shock or analysis paralysis. Don't make them guess what your site is about or you will lose them and they most likely will not return for a second visit.

7. **Social content.** Make sure that you have something "social" on your site, whether it's a blog, forum or even your very own social networking page. The easiest and best of these is a blog in my opinion.

8. **Update often.** Search engines like sites that have a lot of fresh content, this will really help you with ranking in major search engines like Google. If you have a blog you should plan to update it twice weekly at least.

9. **Share and share alike.** Make sure that your content is easy to share. If you don't have sharing widgets on your site (Like this on Facebook, Tweet This!, Digg, Delicious, etc.) then get your designer to add it to the site ASAP. Most blogging software comes with this all ready to go.

10. **Placement and remarketing.** First off, make sure that you understand how people surf, meaning where their eyes go to when they land on a website. The first place is the upper left hand quadrant of a site, that's where your primary message should be placed. Then their eyes go to the center of your site. These two primary places are significant in conversion. You should have a clear message, and a clear call to action

(whatever that action may be). I also recommend funneling your visitors into a mailing list. You can do this via a sign-up on your home page and then an ethical bribe to encourage them to sign up. What's an ethical bribe? It's something you give them (of value) to get something: you might give them an ebook, a checklist or a special report. Just make sure it's something your readers want.

Bonus Tip: Understanding Anchor Text

If you ask any Search Engine Marketing Expert they will tell you the importance of anchor text. So what is this exactly? It's the hyperlinked text that you click on to follow a link. Most people overlook this text, using words like "click here" or other nebulous terms. If used correctly, anchor text can really help with your site ranking. It's not that difficult to implement really, you just need to understand a few basic concepts.

First, anchor text should be descriptive. It should describe the link you're sending people to using keywords that reflect the page you're recommending.

Second, if you know the high traffic keywords for your market you can use those as well to describe the link (but only if the keywords relate to the page you're sending visitors to).

Third, knowing where to use anchor text is almost as important as the text itself. All external links should be anchor text, but often web designers forget internal links (i.e. links leading to pages within your site) although they are equally as important. Your home page is also critical for anchor text links. If you have a blog (and you should) make sure that any article, website or blog you reference has anchor text in the hyperlink.

Creating these hyperlinks is easy, especially if you're using them in a blog. Most blog software has some very simple one-click anchor text creation widgets.

So take some time and go through your site, make sure that anything you have hyperlinked is anchor text. To reiterate: stay away from nebulous terms like "click here" or "follow this link" because you won't get picked up by search engines that way. Make sure the text is focused and specific. How long can anchor text be? It doesn't have to be long, but if need be, it can be multiple words. Keep in mind that as long as the words are relevant to your topic, the anchor text verbiage is all that matters.

5 QUICK WAYS TO REV UP YOUR SITE'S SEARCHABILITY

STRATEGY 13

1. **Content is king, so are keywords.** Find the keywords that people are searching for in your market and then create content around those words.

2. **Don't abuse keywords.** Have you ever seen those sites that seem to use keywords over and over again (i.e. keyword stuffing)? That's an abuse of keywords and while it might temporarily inflate your search engine ranking, it won't last. Once Google figures out what you're doing (and trust me they will) your site ranking will drop drastically. It's not pretty.

3. **Google runs the world.** Well, not really but they certainly do run the Internet. If you're going to optimize your site for ranking make sure that it shows up high on Google, in the end it's the main search engine we default to and the one that matters to your consumer. Studies show that an average website gets 61% of its traffic from search engines, 41% of that from Google alone.

4. **This stuff takes time.** Nothing happens overnight, especially online (unless you're a dancing pancake video that gets sent out to a billion people in a four-hour time span). Ranking and searchability takes times. If you have a book launching in the next three to six months start this work now. You'll be glad you did.

5. **Update your site.** While updating your site in principle might seem like an easy thing, it can be one of the biggest obstacles for a site owner. Why? Because often our website people are overseas and once that 12-year-old from Lithuania goes back to school it's anyone's guess how

to find him. So here's a tip: get a blog, a blog (if updated frequently) will ping the search engines and let them know you have fresh content on your site. Oh and seriously, fire the 12-year-old and hire someone locally. You'll be glad you did.

STRATEGY 14: 10 SECRETS FOR SAVVY SEARCH ENGINE OPTIMIZATION

If you want to get a solid, high ranking in search engines (and who doesn't?), there are a few key things you need to do to make sure your site is helping, and not hurting your ranking. Google tends to dominate searches online (gaining a whopping 63% of all searches) so a lot of what I'm recommending here is based on this search engine's preferences.

Do:

1. Have great content and keep the word count on your home page to somewhere in the 250 word range.

2. Get high quality, high-traffic incoming links from relevant sites.

3. Make sure your website pages have titles, if you're not sure ask your web designer about this.

4. Use good keywords for your home page text. Don't talk about yourself; remember it's about the person landing on your site, not about you.

5. Check out your competition. If you're trying to get incoming links, see who's linking to your competition. How do you search for incoming links? Pop the following into your Google search box: linkdomain:www.website.com

6. Have a focused goal on your home page. While your site can do a good many things (and many sites do), your home page should have one goal. Once you get someone to your website you don't want to confuse them.

A confused mind doesn't make a choice and will likely click off to your competition.

7. Get a good URL, something that relates to your topic and is easy to remember. If you have a few different website addresses (such as your name, maybe an old domain, etc.) make sure they aren't all forwarding to the same page on your site. Have them forward to different pages; this will also help with your search rank.

Don't:

1. Speaking of keywords...try to avoid using slogans, catch phrases or industry jargon. Here's why: First, your reader might be a layperson and doesn't understand what you've written, if you confuse the reader you will lose them. Second, when you search for your site in Google, you'll see that some text comes up with your site URL, this text is pulled from your home page so use that space wisely.

2. Use flash, it's pretty and also pretty annoying. People don't have time to wait for flash loading and also search engines can't spider flash. If you have a flash page as an entrance to your site it's like putting up a brick wall no one can see through. Your site is behind there somewhere but no one will ever find it. Not good.

3. Rely on link farms to get a lot of incoming links. What are link farms? They are services sold with the specific objective of getting incoming links to your site. The problem with these services is they don't care what kind of links they get you as long as it's a link. What this means to you is that you might get a thousand new links to your book on diet and health but they might all be links coming from plumbing sites (I'm not kidding, I've seen this happen).

Search Engine Optimization doesn't have to be complicated or difficult, the thing to remember is that a static, boring site doesn't help your ranking. As a final tip you should also consider getting a blog. If you think blogs are passé think again. A blog, if updated frequently (a minimum of twice weekly) will help your site spider through the search engines and, along with the other tips mentioned above, help you gain ranking and customers.

STRATEGY 15
12 SECRETS TO SELLING MORE BOOKS AT EVENTS

You got a book event, great! Now you want to maximize it, right? You've heard from your writing buddies (or perhaps read online) about the lack of attendance at signings so figuring out how to maximize the event, regardless of the numbers, might be tricky. While I spend a lot of time addressing online marketing, the offline component is one you shouldn't overlook and if book events are where you want to focus, then bringing in some ideas to help you sell more books is something you should consider.

Some years back when I was promoting *The Cliffhanger* I ended up at a book signing in the driving rain, I mean it was pouring and the store was all but empty. It was amazing I sold even one book, let alone seven. While not a big number the copies were all sold to people who were seeking refuge in the store from the rain and not there for my event. This signing taught me a lot about events and connecting with consumers in stores.

If you have an event coming up, consider these ideas before you head out:

1. **Marketing.** First and foremost is the marketing of your event. But I'm not talking about the marketing you do to the media (though that is great too) I'm speaking of in-store marketing, this is what most folks seem to overlook. This is where you supply things to the store to help them market your event. Because the first phase of a successful event is driving people to it. Here are a few thoughts.

    a. **Do bag stuffers.** You can easily do this in your word processing program. Do two per page, meaning that you use one 8 1/2 by 11 sheet of paper to do two fliers. You'll want to ask the store first if they mind that you provide this, most stores or event venues don't.

b. **Bookmarks.** While most in the industry see these as passé, people still love them. You can do bookmarks and bag stuffers (or staple them to the flier) or you can do custom bookmarks with the date and time of your event. Nowadays it's pretty easy to get these done cheaply. Keep in mind that if you are having the event in a mall or other type shopping area, you might be able to drop the bookmarks (or bag stuffers) off at the nearby stores to see if they'll help promote the event.

2. **Book signings are boring.** Regardless of where you do the event plan to do a talk instead of a signing. People are drawn into a discussion and are often turned off by an author just sitting at a table. Marketing is about message and movement so stand up and speak. If speaking in public is intimidating to you, go to Toastmasters or some other local networking/speaking group and see what you can learn.

3. **Unique places.** If you want to get more attention for your event, consider doing events in unique places. We've done them in video stores, electronics stores, gyms, even restaurants (on slow nights), doing outside-the-bookstore events is a great way to gain more interest for your talk. Why? Because you aren't competing with everyone else at the bookstore for your crowd. When you do an event at a locale that doesn't normally do events, you'll gather more people just because it's considered unique.

4. **Show up early and talk it up.** OK so let's say you're in the store and there are a ton of people in there shopping (a book event dream, yes?) I suggest that you take your extra bag stuffers or custom bookmarks and just hand them to the people in the store. Let them know you are doing an event at such and such time and you'd love it if they could sit in. You'll be surprised how many new people you might pull in this way.

5. **Customize.** Regardless of what your talk is about, poll the audience first to see: a) what brought them there, or b) what they hope to learn if your talk is educational. I suggest this because the more you can customize your discussion the more likely you are to sell a book. If you can solve problems (and this is often done during the Q&A) all the better. You'll look like the answer machine you are and readers love that. If you have the answers they'll want to buy from you. I promise.

6. **Make friends.** Get to know the bookstore people, but not just on the

day of the event. Go in prior and make friends, tell them who you are and maybe even hand them your flier or bookmark (or a stack if you can). Often stores have Information Centers, see if you can leave some fliers there instead of just at the register. Getting to know the people who are selling the book is a great way to help gather more people to your event. If your event isn't in a bookstore but attached to a shopping area or mall, go around to the stores (and perhaps you did this when you passed out the fliers) and let them know you have an event, ask what can you do to help them promote it. If you can rally the troops to help you market your talk, you could triple the number of people at your event. No kidding.

7. **Take names.** I always, always recommend that you get names and email addresses from the folks who attend. Signing them up for your mailing list is a great way to stay in touch with them and stay on your reader's radar screen. If you have a giveaway or drawing, great! This will help you to collect names. If you don't, offer them a freebie or ebook after the event. Often if I'm doing a PowerPoint presentation I will put together a set of them (delivered in PDF) after the event. Attendees need to sign up to get them and then once they do, I include them in our newsletter list, which helps me to stay on their radar screen.

8. **Pricing.** Make sure your book is easy to buy. If you are doing this outside of a bookstore this is easy to do and will help your sales. I find that a rounded number like $10 or $20 makes for a quick and easy sale. If you can round up or down without adding or losing too much to the price, by all means do it.

9. **Book pairing.** One way you might be able to round up is by pairing your book with a freebie. When I paired *Red Hot Internet Publicity* with a second, but smaller, marketing book I took the awkward pricing of $18.95, bumped it up to $20 (so 2 books for $20) and quadrupled my sales after an event. Now the pairing doesn't have to be a book, it can be a special report or even an ebook that you send to them after the event.

10. **Product and placement.** As you're doing your talk (especially if it's in a non-bookstore venue) make sure that you have a copy of the book propped up in front of you so event visitors see it the entire time you are speaking. Hold up the book when appropriate and use it as an example

when you can. This will help to direct the consumer's eye to the book—and making eye contact with the product is a good way to make sure it stays on their radar screen throughout your talk. When I do a speaking gig at an event that allows me to sell books in the room, I will sell four times more than I would if the attendees have to go somewhere else to buy it, so make the buy easy. If you can, make sure your books are for sale in the room.

11. **Ease of purchase.** Aside from pricing, if you're doing your own checkout make sure that you have many ways consumers can buy your book. I take credit cards at the event, checks and cash. Don't limit yourself as to what you can take or you will limit your sales.

11. **Post event wrap up.** So the event is over, what now? Well, if you got attendees to sign up for your newsletter (you did do that, right?) now it's time to send a thank you note for attending and remind them (if they missed the chance at the event) to buy a copy of your book at the "special event price."

Speaking and book events are great ways to build your platform, but if you aren't selling books there's little point in doing them. For many of us, our book is our business card and thus, if we can sell our "business card" we can keep consumers in our funnel. If your book isn't your business card you still want readers, right? The marketing both pre and during an event is crucial to building your readership. While it's easy to say that events sell books, they often don't. I find that if you don't "work it" you often will find your time wasted. Seek the opportunities when they are made available to you and then maximize them, you'll be glad you did!

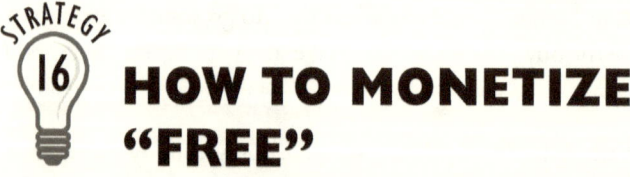

STRATEGY 16
HOW TO MONETIZE "FREE"

These days, everyone talks about free content. "Give it away!" they say, but does this really work? Well, yes and no. As with anything, there has to be a strategy.

On a morning run through my neighborhood I noticed a number of garage sale signs (that's tag sale for those of you back east). One of the signs had a sign beneath it that read: We have free stuff! As I ran though the neighborhood I passed that house and noticed they put all their free stuff in the "Free zone" and already, even at that early hour, hoards of people were migrating there. I passed the other garage sales, which were doing OK, but not great. Clearly the one with the free stuff pulled more people, but did it actually sell more paid merchandise? Yes. I checked in with the sale after my run to find most of the good stuff gone (note to self: shop first, exercise later). When I talked to the homeowner he said that the free stuff went fast, but as I noted each time I passed by, it wasn't junk stuff, it was actually good enough to make the garage sale shopper feel like they got a real deal. If it's junk and it's free, it doesn't really matter.

What's the lesson here? Free stuff can help you sell more of the paid merchandise, but you have to be careful, because some people just want freebies and that's fine. But they are not your customers.

Here are some tips to help you maximize the use of free:

1. **Why free?** The first question you should ask yourself is why are you doing this? If you aren't sure, then free might not be right for you. Free content should be offered to help further your message, build a list, and get new people into your marketing funnel. If your model isn't set up

this way, maybe it should be. If you aren't interested in this kind of a marketing model, then free probably isn't your thing.

2. **Define how free can help.** Figure out why you want to give free stuff. As I mentioned above, getting clear about your model will help determine if a free product is even worth your time. If it is, then you need to figure out how it will help you. As an example, we have a lot of free stuff on the Author Marketing Experts, Inc. site (www.ameauthors.com) but the free for us is designed to build trust. Distrust is rampant online, and in particular, in the book promotion and publishing industry. There are a lot of scams out there and so trust is important. Our free stuff builds our mailing list, yes, but it also builds trust.

3. **Make sure it's really free.** A lot of people have content that is purported to be free when it's not really free. What I mean is that you get a sliver of it, not even a piece really worth mentioning, but the stuff you want is something you have to pay for. If you want to do free, make it free. Find something of value and give it to your customers.

4. **Make it something your end user wants.** As I've mentioned a few times, make sure the free is something people want. If it isn't, you: a) won't bring in the right crowd of people (you'll end up just getting the freebie hunters, and b) you won't build your mailing list as fast. So, for example, give your readers something really substantial like an ebook or tips, or a workbook. Virtually any electronic product is easy to create and deliver. When I changed our freebie on the Author Marketing Experts, Inc. website, we quadrupled our sign-ups. So, what was the freebie? *52 Ways to Sell More Books*. Now, as an author, isn't that appealing to you? Exactly my point.

5. **What if you've written a fiction book?** Well, consider this: 83% of Americans want to write a book, so what if you gave them a free how-to guide? You don't even have to create this yourself, you could partner with someone who has already created one. If you don't like that idea, consider (for those of you in the historical fiction market) doing a did-you-know piece on the history you're referencing in your book. The idea here is to: a) give value and b) give your readers something they will care about. Also, whenever possible, give your readers something they need to keep so it will remind them of you and your book: tip sheets,

workbooks, and reference charts. All of these things are pieces that your consumer may keep, which can keep you top of mind.

6. **Take names.** You should never give free away without asking for an email address. I see people do this all the time; they have a ton of free stuff but never collect emails. If that's the case, the freebies you are offering may be of great value to your end user but they won't matter to your marketing. Get emails. It's called an ethical bribe. You get something (their email) and give them something (the free stuff).

7. **Make it easy to get.** Don't make free difficult. If people have to jump through hoops, they won't do it and the free stuff won't matter. Put your free stuff on your home page, or at least have a link to it, though I recommend using free stuff as an ethical bribe (as a way to get sign-ups for your newsletter). When you ask for their email, make it easy. A simple click or two is all it should take. Then, don't ask for too much information. If you ask me for my address, birthday and whatnot I doubt I will want your free stuff that badly. Shorten the staircase. If you make it complicated, it's not really free. Just bait. If you bait your consumer in this fashion you'll lose them.

8. **Make the free stuff work for you.** If you give away something, make sure that it works for you. What I mean is that when you get our free stuff, we always make sure and remind folks of who we are and what we do. For a while we had a free Twitter ebook that always went out with our product catalog imbedded in it.

9. **Call to action.** Make sure your free stuff has a call to action. You are collecting names and email addresses and building your list, that's great. But what do you really want people to do? Define what you want them to do, and then include your call to action in the free stuff. Let's face it, it's a good piece—designed to help your reader—but it must also help you. It's ok to promote your book on the last page, or encourage folks to do a consult with you if that's what you offer. You can also offer specials and change these periodically in the giveaway.

10. **What will you give?** People often ask me what you should give away, and I say, it depends. Who is your market and what do they want? Now, on our site you'll see *52 Ways to Sell More Books,* which is an ebook we offer when you sign up for our newsletter. Do our folks want that? You bet.

Why? Because they are authors and authors want to sell more books. A special report or ebook always makes a great freebie, maybe you have a white paper that you did on the industry; if so, offer it as a freebie.

11. **Follow up!** The best kind of free stuff is, as I like to call it, the gift that keeps giving. Auto responders are a great system but often underutilized when it comes to marketing. If you are collecting names and then never contacting your prospects again, what's the point? Our *52 Ways to Sell More Books* is delivered over several weeks, and then when we're done, we deliver more quality content. People need to be reminded, and reminded again. Now, you can also funnel folks into your newsletter as I mentioned earlier. I do both. We have the auto responder and the newsletter. Think it's too much? Maybe, but our market wants information. Define what your market wants and then give it to them. If a newsletter and an auto responder is overkill, then scale it back. No one knows your market like you do.

The real key here is that free stuff can work well for you in so many ways, but free stuff without a goal is just free. Great to get free stuff, right? But then how is all of this hard work going to pay off for you?

If you still aren't a believer of free, try it for 90 days and see if it doesn't change your life. If you do it right, free will monetize your audience like nothing else will. The biggest reason is that in an age of pushing things on consumers, your audience really wants to sample what you have to offer before they buy. Free is a great way to do that. It's also a great way to stay in front of your audience, build trust, and develop a loyal following.

We Love Free Stuff

If 2009 was the year of discounts then 2010 and beyond is likely to be the year(s) of free stuff, this according to ChiefMarketer.com's 2010 prospecting survey. Here's how the survey broke down: 88.1% want free gifts, 93% want free shipping, and a whopping 94.5% want free content i.e. ebooks, goodies, webinars, etc. What does this mean for you? Sweeten the pot. When we ran our special of buying my book, **Red Hot Internet Publicity** with a second, free book, book sales tripled. No kidding. (See: http://bit.ly/cl3O1m). Try pairing your book with a goodie and see how much your sales increase.

STRATEGY 17: AFFILIATE MARKETING

If you have an e-commerce-enabled website and you're selling products like ebooks and other electronic downloads, an affiliate marketing program can be a powerful way to generate serious traffic and sales. You can create an affiliate marketing program to incentivize other websites to market your products to their visitors in exchange for a referral fee. They earn a commission, and you increase your exposure and expand your customer base.

To implement your affiliate marketing program:

1. Create a landing page (a web page that communicates the features and benefits of the product). If your products are strictly digital, meaning there's no physical package to ship, then you'll probably go with a service like ClickBank (http://www.clickbank.com). If you're going to be shipping physical product to the customer, you can utilize an existing program like DirectTrack (http://www.directtrack.com) or MyAffiliateProgram (http://www.myaffiliateprogram.com).

2. Create affiliate marketing tools (email copy, small ads, etc.) that your affiliates can use to sell your product.

3. Compile a list of potential affiliates and contact them via email to invite them to join your affiliate program.

Leverage Amazon.com's Associate Program: if your book is the only product you're selling on your personal website, I'd encourage you to send your visitors to Amazon.com (through their affiliate program) to purchase your book. There are many advantages to using Amazon.com rather than filling the book orders in-house: they are masters at e-commerce and have defined the online purchasing experience (especially for books), you can eliminate the hassle of filling orders in-house, and most people are already comfortable purchasing books from Amazon.com, which increases the likelihood that they will complete their orders. To join Amazon.com's Associate Program, go to http://www.amazon.com and click on "Join Associates."

Why sell one book when you can sell 10,000? The potential revenue generated from bulk book orders is scintillating: although these thousand-dollar orders require you to heavily discount your book, the possibility of infusing so many copies of your book into the marketplace in one simple transaction is wonderful... and often possible.

A number of bulk sales opportunities are available, including book clubs, network marketing organizations, and mail order catalogs. Book clubs alone represent a billion-dollar market for publishers. There are numerous ways to structure deals with book clubs [see John Kremer's 1001 Ways to Market Your Books (Open Horizons, 2000) for more information].

Here are a few resources to get you started:
- Book-of-the-Month, Inc.: http://www.bomc.com (They operate over ten book clubs and have over 3.5 million members.)
- Books Are Fun: http://www.booksarefun.com (a division of Reader's Digest that places bulk orders for a select few books)

Literary Marketplace: The Directory of the American Book Publishing Industry with Industry Yellowpages (Information Today, 2001) has a complete listing of book clubs you can contact.

STRATEGY 18: THE BLOG FACTOR: EVERYTHING YOU NEED TO KNOW TO START BLOGGING—TODAY!

What is this blog factor? Well, what a few thought was a novel idea some years ago has now morphed into something no one expected. There are currently nine million blogs out there with 40,000 new ones being added every day. Some are informative and some are just downright a waste of your time. And while we hear a lot about blogging these days, what is blogging really? Blogging in its simplest term is like an online journal but much, much more powerful. Blogs (short for web log) is a place where surfers can get up to the minute information on a topic or take a peek into someone's life. Some blogs are nothing more than a daily glimpse into a private world, while others are so sophisticated it's hard to tell them apart from an online news service.

Why Blogs Matter

Google, the #1 search engine on the Net, loves blogs. So much so that if you do it right Google will spider the heck out of your site. What does it mean to spider? Well spidering is when Google, or the like, searches your site's content to establish ranking, the more content you have (i.e. fresh content) the more Google will do its magic and push your site up the search engine rankings. Another reason blogs matter is that they are interactive and, if you blog on your product, service or area of expertise, it will help to further your expert status on a particular issue. When we plan our virtual promotion for our clients, we include as many blogs as we can into a tour. Why? Because if you can get into a good blog that's seeing a lot of traffic, you can really start to gain some exposure for your product, service or message.

What Would You Talk About?

This is the question we get asked most often. "If I start a blog, what on earth would I talk about?"

Here are a few ideas to get you started:
- Talk about trends
- Review other products in your market
- Blog about new developments either within your company or in the industry
- Lend your "voice" to a hot issue
- Comment on or feature other blogs
- Interview people in your industry
- Talk about the elephant in the room (meaning talk about the thing that no one wants to talk about, this could be an emerging trend or a market change that's affecting your industry)

Keep in mind that there's nothing wrong with controversy. Remember that you want to create your own voice, your own take on a certain issue and if that opinion is controversial, all the better for exposure and for getting people to interact on your blog. Getting readers to respond to your posts is a great way to gain interest and momentum for your blog and (more importantly) getting people to talk about it will grow your blog like nothing else!

How to Start a Blog

Starting a blog is super easy. All you have to do is register at a blog site (like www.wordpress.org or www.blogger.com) and get started. It's that easy. The blog service will link to your site; you'll need to ask your Webmaster to add a button to your home page so people can find your blog.

How to Blog Effectively

The best bloggers know that the more you add to your blog, the more traffic you'll drive there. Some bloggers I know post daily, sometimes even multiple times a day while others post weekly. How much you post will probably depend on how much time you have to dedicate to this, the challenge will be that if you want to keep driving people to your blog, you'll want fresh content.

This doesn't mean you have to create this all yourself, in fact you can invite people onto your blog and interview them, or you can just post a one paragraph "thought" on your topic. It doesn't have to be complicated or long, it just has to be fresh. Also be innovative, as we discussed earlier, be different with your blog, have fun with it. It might seem complicated at first but once you get the hang of it, you'll quickly become a blog expert!

STRATEGY 19: 10 REASONS WHY YOU SHOULD BE BLOGGING

With all the Tweeting, Facebook Liking, and LinkedIn connecting going on, it's easy to forget about blogging and finding the time to do so. Blogging, however, can be extremely useful for more reasons than just populating your website with content (although that's important too).

Let's look at some reasons why you must blog and why it should matter to you!

Blogging gives "voice" to a website: In an age where there are millions of websites and millions more coming online each month, how can you stand apart from the crowd? One way is to get a great looking site, but as we all know, sometimes budgets allow just the basics. A blog can then step in and (through your voice) give content and character to any website, regardless of how fancy or plain it might be. In fact, some of the best blogs have carried the success of many a less-than-spectacular website.

Content marketing: We all know that we need to create content and lots of it, but who has the time? Well, now you can use your blog as a content creating machine. You can develop original content there and push it out to different areas. For example, I will sometimes use my blog posts for Twitter updates, Facebook updates, and article syndication.

Search engine candy: Blogs are great optimization tools. Search engines (especially Google) love sites that are updated frequently. One easy and quick way to do that is via a blog. Each time you update your blog it pings the search engines and tells them the content on your site has been updated.

Social media must: If you're going to Tweet, or want to be liked on Facebook, there's no two ways about it, you must have a blog. That's the site you send them to for your complete content, where they can comment, become a follower and help you grow your tribe.

Blogger friendly: If you're going to pitch bloggers, you must first have a blog. Love bloggers? Be a blogger first. Similar to the step above, you can become active on other blogs, commenting and sharing ideas, and attract them back to yours where they can return the favor. By the time you pitch them, you're not just another email in an inbox, you're someone they know and like.

Be an industry leader: It's hard to be a leader in the industry if you don't have a voice. A blog can give you a voice. Also, by blogging on your market, you can stay in touch with your market and hot topics much easier. Stay dialed in, stay current: a blog can help you do that.

Media, speaking: I've gotten media interviews and speaking gigs from my blog. If you blog enough and on interesting, relevant issues, you can gain some serious momentum for not only your website, but your career as well.

The competitive edge: No matter what category you publish under, there is always a lot of competition. Yes, you can compete with a better cover, a better book, but on your website a blog will help define you as the author in a unique way that a book category can't. When you're in a cluttered market, like dating, dieting or finance, a blog can really help to define and refine your message.

Credibility: Blogs are great credibility builders. Getting on topic and giving your opinion (and yes, being different) can really help to build your footing and credibility in the marketplace.

Site traffic/SEO: Aside from what a blog can do for your site as it relates to Google, an active blog can also help to increase site traffic and help further optimize the site. It's a fantastic tool for getting your site better links, traffic and a higher ranking in search engines.

So now that I've convinced you to blog, I want to refer you to another piece I've written on blogging called "How to Become a Powerhouse Blogger in 15 Minutes" I hope that this piece, along with the tips provided above, will help you launch or reinvigorate your blogging campaign.

STRATEGY 20: THE REAL SECRET TO TWITTER

If you've ever been impressed by the number of followers someone has on Twitter, I have a newsflash for you: it doesn't matter. The thing is, you can buy followers (no, I'm not kidding) sort of like buying mailing lists. How effective is buying followers? Well, let me ask you: how effective was the last mailing list you bought? Whatever your answer is I can guarantee you that buying Twitter followers will be far less effective. Why? Because social media does not favor automation, it favors engagement, interaction, and yes, being social. You might be interested in knowing someone's Twitter-reach or you might be trying to determine if your campaign is effective.

Here are some key things to look at when measuring anyone's Twitter success:

1. How active is the person on Twitter?
2. How relevant to their market are their updates? For example did a mystery author just tell you she's washing her cat?
3. How much do they broadcast vs. communicate?
4. How often are they retweeted?
5. How many Twitter lists are they on?

One of the best ways to determine if your Twitter campaign is effective—or someone else's is—is by gauging how often they are retweeted. Retweeting is an important factor in Twitter, possibly the most significant means to determine an effective Twitter person from an ineffective one. In fact, Twitter popularity lists aren't based on the amount of followers but rather on the amount of activity in a campaign. When I recently pulled up a list of the top 10 Tweeters in Southern California, I found that many in the top 10 didn't even break 10,000 followers.

How can you determine how active an account is? There are a few services that you might want to look into. The first is Retweet Rank (retweetrank.com). This service shows you (by user) how much someone has been retweeted as well as their most popular retweeted posts.

Twitter Analyzer (twitteranalyzer.com) is another great tool for determining how far tweets have traveled. You can isolate a user or a particular Twitter-stream. Very useful site!

How can you increase your tweet-ability?

Here are a few tips to help you grow your Twitter campaign:

Know what your followers want: The first piece sounds simple but could take you the most amount of time. Candidly, it took me three months to finally get a handle on what my followers wanted and what seemed to rank high on the retweeting scale. If you don't know what your followers want, try following popular people in your market and see what they are posting about. Use this as a guideline to help you dig deeper into what your market wants.

Share useful advice: Now that you've determined what your followers want to see on Twitter, make sure the information you are sharing is helpful. I know this sounds like an oxymoron. If you've determined what your followers want of course what you Tweet on will be helpful, right? Wrong. Ask yourself what they need, not what you think they want. There is a big difference.

Don't overtweet: OK, full confession, I've been guilty of this from time to time but now I've found a good balance of between 4 and 5 posts a day. This may be a metric that works for you, but you'll need to determine that on your own. How do you know? If people start unfollowing you, the reason may be because you are overtweeting.

Balance broadcasting with communicating: This is a biggie for many of us. It's important to use any social media tool like a telephone. You would never call someone and just blast them with information, right? You'll give them something, wait for a response and then respond to their question and so a discussion ensues. Use social media as you would a telephone: communicate, don't broadcast.

Comment on current events that relate to your industry: Becoming the go-to person for everything related to your industry is what most of us aspire to. Keeping apprised of what's going on in your industry is important and then, sharing the highlights or most significant items with your followers will go a long way toward growing your popularity.

Recommend helpful resources: Much like current events, you want to offer helpful resources to your followers. This might not be appropriate to every market, but for the majority of us this works very well. Again, the more you can become a resource the more you will grow your popularity on Twitter or, for that matter, any social media site.

Many people hop onto Twitter thinking it's a numbers game when it really isn't. You can have a Twitter-tribe of millions and not gain the same kind of social media success that you would with only 1,000 followers. The wisdom of the crowd knows that it's not always the size of the audience that matters but how engaged they are in you and your message. Find the balance that works for. You'll be glad you did.

How many writers Tweet?

According to TweepSearch queries, there are 1,790 novelists, 9,139 poets, 19,490 journalists 28,529 authors, and a staggering 99,082 writers on Twitter.

See MediaBistro for the full article: http://www.mediabistro.com/galleycat/twitter/literary_twitter_census_147251.asp.

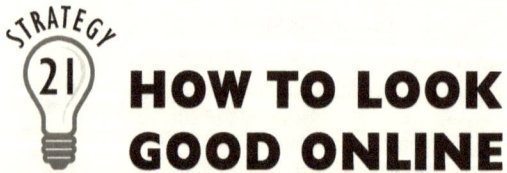

HOW TO LOOK GOOD ONLINE

There are those that say it's all about appearances, this is very true online. Why? Because everything you do online not only leaves a footprint but it's also your 24/7 resume. If the footprint you're leaving looks unprofessional and half-finished, it might not bode well for your online reputation and sales.

Here are some quick tips on how to look good online:

Social Networks: With social networks it's not about quantity but quality. I often have authors tell me they are on numerous social networking sites (some are on as many as 50). That's great if you can keep them all current, but not if you can't find the ones you can participate in and stick with those. Remember that the first word in social networking is "social" so if you're not able to participate actively (at least once a week) then get out.

Sign up for Google alerts: Who's saying what about you? If you don't know you should. This is (usually) a good thing. You want to know where reviews appear so you can: a) link to them and b) thank the person who reviewed you or mentioned you on their blog or website.

Get a blog: In order to get on blogs, you must have a blog, but it's more than just having one, it's about keeping it updated (see Participate).

Participate: In order to reap the benefits of the online world you must participate. This goes back to the social networking site and your blog. Participate, communicate and listen. Three rules online that will never steer you wrong.

Don't get greedy: Lead with the benefits, not the dollar signs. What I mean by this is that if you're going online to make a quick buck, get out. You might make a few dollars but success will be short lived.

Network: It goes without saying that networking (especially online) is important. Network, lend a helping hand, show people how you can help them.

Website: Don't just get one, get a good one. You'd never think to show up for a car race with a scooter. Don't even try to go online with anything less than a professional website. While I know it's tempting to do it yourself most authors always end up regretting it. "My website is fine," they'll say until you ask them how well it's selling for them. If the answer is: "It's not," then you need a new site. Show up online with a site that reflects your expertise, creativity, and message. This is one race you can't afford to lose.

STRATEGY 22
12 THINGS AUTHORS DO TO SABOTAGE THEIR SUCCESS

Writing, publishing, promoting, publicizing. It all seems quite daunting, doesn't it? Well, it doesn't have to be. First you need to start out by doing the right things and knowing what can help, or harm, your success. Keep in mind that while there is always a creative element, publishing is a business. It's important to know your business to be successful. Here are a dozen ideas that I hope will help you on your journey from writer to successful author.

1. **Waiting too long to market.** When it comes to marketing, some authors wait too long to get the word out there. If you're sitting on top of your publication date wondering where to start with your marketing, you're about six months behind the curve. Book marketing is what I call the long runway of promotion. A great campaign will consist not only of a focused marketing plan, but a plan that starts early enough to support the ramp up that a good book marketing campaign needs. And this isn't just for the self-published market, any book that's being released these days needs a minimum of a six-month ramp up. This doesn't mean that you are marketing during that time, but ideally you are getting ready for your launch by having a website designed, starting a newsletter, building your mailing list, building your media list, planning your events, etc.

2. **Not having enough money.** I see it all the time; authors spend all their money on the book process (book cover, editing, etc.) and then don't have enough for the marketing. That's like opening up a store and not having money to stock it with inventory. Before you jump headlong into publishing a book, make sure you have the funds to do so. So, how much is enough? It depends on what you want to accomplish. Be clear on your goals and market, then sit down with someone who can help you determine a budget.

3. **Not getting to know others in their market.** Who else is writing about your topic? If you're not sure, then you should do your research. Getting to know your fellow genre authors is not only important, but it can really help you with your marketing. How? Because most readers don't just buy one self-help book, or one dating book, they will generally buy in multiples. So getting to know others within your market can not only help you market your book, but it could also help you connect with fellow authors, and there is truth to the fact that there is power in numbers.

4. **Ignoring social media.** While social media may seem confusing to most of us, it's important to know that it can sometimes be a make or break situation when it comes to marketing your book. If you can't make heads or tails out of Twitter vs. Facebook, then hire someone who can help you or guide you through your choices.

5. **Thinking bookstores don't matter.** While it's nice to think that most of us do our shopping online and via Amazon, bookstores (especially local stores) can really help or hurt your marketing efforts. If your book isn't going into bookstores, then you'll want to get to know your local area stores to see if you can present your book to them for consideration and/or do an event in their store. Having a local presence in bookstores is important, especially if you are doing local events and local media. If the bookstore won't stock the book (and many of them won't if you're a first time author), then make sure at the very least that your book can be ordered. You don't want people walking into your neighborhood store and being told "Sorry, we can't get that book."

6. **Printing too many copies.** In order to get large printing discounts, authors will often print huge numbers of their books. I've seen ranges from 10,000 on up. Generally I recommend a run of no more than 2,000. You can always go back to print and likely when you do, you'll want to make changes to the book, possibly adding new testimonials, endorsements, and reviews. Also, you have better things to do with your marketing dollars than spend them on storage space.

7. **Not spending enough time researching their market.** If you were going to open up a store in a mall, let's say a yogurt shop, would you ever consider opening a store without doing the proper research? Probably not. Yet every day authors publish books and haven't done market

research. This research, while it can be tedious, could save you hundreds of dollars in promotion and/or cover design.

8. **Not hiring a professional to do their book cover.** In tight financial times, it's ok to cut corners in marketing or find less expensive ways to do things. But one corner you shouldn't cut is on your book cover. Your cover is important because it's the first impression your audience has of your book. Don't shortcut your success by creating a cover that doesn't sell. In the long run, the money you save on the cover design could cost you four times that in book sales.

9. **Not having their work professionally edited.** Your book is your resume; not only that but it's your reader's experience as well. What kind of experience do you want to give them? If the answer is a great one (and it likely is) make sure the work you do on your book mirrors that. Your work should always be professionally edited, no excuse. If you don't have enough money to do this, then ask yourself if publishing this book is really a good idea. Perhaps waiting until you have the funds to get the book released the right way is a better idea.

10. **Expecting immediate book sales.** Nothing happens immediately, especially book sales. The sales process for books can be lengthy, especially when you're dealing with multiple reporting agencies. Most authors don't know that places like Amazon, Baker & Taylor, and Ingram don't all pay on the same timeframe. They all have particular cycles to how they pay. For example, Amazon might pay 90 days after the sale, whereas some folks I've talked to say that Baker & Taylor sometimes lags five months behind. What this means is that if you are pushing your book in December and hope to see the fruits of your labor in January, that timeline isn't realistic. Don't end up disappointed if your royalty statements aren't reflecting the promotion you've done. It could be that the agencies just haven't caught up with your sales.

11. **Not having a website.** Someone once asked me if all authors should have a website, to which I responded: does your book need a book cover? Every author should have a website. It doesn't have to be fancy, lengthy, or expensive, but it's a 24/7 sales tool and the only way to build credibility online.

12. **Giving up on their book too soon.** Like anything, book marketing takes time. I see authors all the time who start to grow impatient after a few months, wondering where their success is. How long will it take? That depends. But you might not be the best person to determine that. If you've been marketing your book for a while and can't figure out why nothing has taken off, spend an hour with a professional who can tell you if you're on the right track. Do this before you decide to throw in the towel. You might be inches away from success; don't give up before you do your research.

Making headway in marketing is as much about the good decisions, as it is avoiding the bad. Good luck in your publishing journey!

STRATEGY 23: NEVER SELL YOUR BOOK

You're all ready to promote your book. You've got a great press kit, a polished bio, and a letter-perfect press release. Now you're ready to sell, sell, sell, right? Wrong. One of the biggest mistakes authors make is selling their book. Remember it's not about the book; it's about what the book can do for the reader.

Finding the benefits to your book might seem like a pretty simple task, but touting that "It's a great read!" won't get you very far. To determine what your book will do for your reader, you'll have to dig deep, sometimes deeper than you thought. Especially if your book is fiction, the task of finding benefits will require some serious brainstorming. The key here is be different. If you have a diet book, don't offer the same benefits a million other books do: you'll lose weight. Instead, offer a benefit that is decidedly different than anything that's out there. Or, try to couch a similar benefit in a different way. At the end of the day, it's all about the WIIFM factor: what's in it for me? If your reader likes what's in it for them, they'll buy your book—otherwise they'll just move on.

The idea of not selling your book also holds true when you're doing an interview. Never, ever answer an interviewer's question with: "You'll find it in my book." Because the fact is, you're an author, of course the answer is in your book, but right now you're there to help them with their interview—save the sales pitches for another time.

The uniqueness of your benefits can also directly relate to the particular audience you're speaking to. For example, if you have different levels of readers or readers from different backgrounds, it's a good idea to work up a set of benefits for each of them. Then any interview you do (or speaking engagement) will offer benefits with that audience in mind as opposed to a more generic form of, "Here's what my book can do for you!" Creating a list of benefits for your book can aid your campaign in a number of ways: first, it'll help you get away from a more "salesy" type of approach, and second, it will help you create the tip sheets that can add substance to your press kit. If you're working on the benefit angle of your book early enough, you can incorporate these into the back copy of your book cover.

The point is, never, ever sell your book. Be a step ahead of the competition and sell what your book can do for the reader, and let them know why it's better than the competition. In the end, that's all anyone will care about.

STRATEGY 24: THE POWER OF SOCIAL NETWORKS

These days, you can't go into a coffee shop, bookstore, or turn on your television without hearing about social networks like Facebook and Squidoo. These sites have exploded in recent years with members and an influx of money that's kept them growing.

The idea behind social networks isn't a new thing, but the concept of socializing online developed and morphed as more and more people spent time in front of their computers. The idea being that you could socialize, network, gather, communicate and meet friends in an online venue, rather than, let's say a coffee shop. Years ago, before social networks, we met people in clubs, organizations, bowling leagues. We may not have had "profiles" like we do on these social networking sites but the concept was still the same: like attracts like and similar interest-based people gathered in places that supported these common interests.

As we continue to delve into this Web 2.0 world, you'll start to see more niche social networking sites like those built for wine lovers, car lovers and book lovers. The more focused a site can get, the more the network expands. And how many sites should you be on? As many as are appropriate to your message and you have time to manage. If you've got a book about cars then by all means, join the car lover's network. Got a book about travel? There's a travel lovers social network as well (we've listed a few of these niche networks further in this chapter).

Social networks, also referred to as social media, are places where people can join and become members of an online community. And why does this matter? Well, for a few reasons. First off, consider the Internet one big networking party. As such, you really want to participate, right? So you show up at the networking party (in this case Facebook or Squidoo) and you network. Meaning you connect with others who are interested in what you are doing.

And much like a real-time networking event, you give first and ask for the sale later. In fact, in most cases you don't even ask for it. If you give enough, eventually you'll make the sale.

People join social networks for a variety of reasons: to socialize, share and/or self-promote. The one caveat to this is that social networks are not receptive to marketing messages or sales hype, but those sitting on these sites are looking for answers and advice. In fact, your presence on a social networking site should be 80 percent education and 20 percent sales. Users on social networking sites want friends, mentors, experts and guidance. If you can offer this to a social networking site or sites, you can certainly grow your list.

The Right Way to Approach a Social Networking Site

There's an old saying that goes: "Fake it till you make it." This is not true of social networking. You can't fake anything. The best sites are those with an authentic voice. Social network members can sense an individual who is pretending to be just an "average Joe" but is really just looking for a quick sale. The worst thing you can do is constantly promote your book.

Users join social media sites to socialize, learn and get to know what you're offering. Be helpful or be gone. That's the motto of the social networks. Remember that social media (much like anything on the Internet) is a trust-based model. You gain trust by helping, advising, educating or enlightening your readers. Seth Godin, who started one of the best social networking sites out there today (Squidoo.com) is a great example of what to do when promoting yourself. He offers helpful advice, tips and insights but rarely promotes his book. Does he sell books? You bet he does, but he's helpful first, and a sales person second (sethgodin.typepad.com). The point is, gain someone's trust and you'll probably gain a sale, too.

Tips for Social Networking Sites

The first piece of this is to figure out what your message will be online. If you're going to expose details of your brand, book, business or life, figure out what you want to expose or, I should say, what's necessary to expose in order to get your message across. This is important because once you start branding yourself on the Net via social networks, you want to be consistent.

Next, remember that the first word in social networks is "social." That being said, these networks only work if you interact with them. Whenever appropriate (and this will vary from network to network), join groups, be sociable, be interactive. Participate. You can't just show up at a party and sit in the corner. Well, you can, but you probably won't get asked back.

If you can spend a half an hour to an hour or so a day on your networks, that's great. Don't overdo the time you spend on them or you'll burn yourself out. If you can use the social network feeds to have them syndicate your blog to the site, the updating of your social networking page will be done for you. To a greater degree, anyway. You'll still want to get in there and tinker, update content, add friends, etc.

Fan Pages and Facebook

Since Facebook is the dominating force out there, let's talk for a moment about Fan Pages. Why would you want one? Well first, you're in the business of marketing and as such, Fan Pages are business pages, so you'll really want to consider pulling your book followers off of your profile and sending them to your Fan Page. Also, Fan Pages are indexed and searched by Google so you'll get great ranking with a Fan Page, more so than you would with a Profile.

Fan Pages, once you know your focus and message, are easy to create and update. You just want to stay on message and know what your followers want.

Tips for Effective Social Networking

Leverage other social media: If you have a strong presence other social networking sites like Twitter or YouTube, then I recommend that you use those sites to promote your Facebook Fan Page. Let folks know where to find you and never, ever forget to add "Follow Me" buttons to your website pages and your blog.

Tagging: You can drive more interest to your page by tagging an author or a popular Facebook page to a status update, photo or video. It's easy to do this in Facebook, you can also tag an article that a high profile member ran on their page.

Step outside of your social circle: Try getting away from your inner circle and migrating out to other people who might be good networking opportunities. While it's fun to stay connected to all your college buddies, that's not the main focus of your Facebook Fan Page.

Selling on Facebook: Facebook now has an application that can add a store page to your Facebook Fan Page. What this means is that you can start selling your books and products from your Fan Page.

Slow and steady wins the social media race: The best Facebook pages (and this is true for any social networking site) are built over time. Slow growth is best when it comes to social networking sites, so don't force a sudden surge of growth. This will also keep you from getting booted off if you add friends too quickly. Facebook watches for people who are adding hundreds of friends at a time and will lock your page if they think you're over-promoting yourself.

Don't be shy: The purpose of Facebook is to connect and interact with other members, so don't be shy! Interact with people on your friend list by commenting on their news, and pictures, and/or wishing them a happy birthday. Doing all these things will help others to get to know who you actually are instead of just knowing your name.

Content, content, content: Remember that it's important to add content. You can do this by uploading a video, adding the RSS feed from your blog and a variety of other things.

Keep updating your Page or Profile: Don't let your profile get stale. Update your status, add photos and answer wall posts and messages.

Add your Facebook page to your blog: Make sure and add your Facebook page to your blog. You can have your web person take care of this for you; it's a simple widget that gets added to let people know you have a Facebook profile.

Social media is a great way to market yourself and your book. When Facebook is integrated with other social networking platforms like Twitter, YouTube and Squidoo, it can be an enormous boon to your inbound marketing campaign. Just remember, your website needs to convert the folks you're sending there.

STRATEGY 25: 14 WAYS TO MAKE YOUR FACEBOOK PAGE FUN & LIVELY

Congratulations! Now you have a Facebook Page, but that's just the beginning.

Unlike a profile, which can and should be personal, a Page can be used to promote you and your book since it has fewer restrictions (such as number of followers). You can connect with your audience, conduct promotions and participate in real-time conversations. Pages offer a lot of great options, including the means to post photos and videos from events, the ability to create groups and a means to publicize events and allow attendees to RSVP.

The first question is usually the same, however: what should I do now?

Let the world know you have a Facebook Page!

- Make sure you have a Facebook widget on your website and blog so it's clear that you have a fanpage and people can click on the widget and get to your Fan Page. There is also a "share" button on the bottom left of your Fan Page that allows you to send the page to your Facebook friends and/or post the Fan Page to your own Facebook profile.

- If you have a personal Facebook page, be sure to "like" your Fan Page.

- If you have an e-newsletter or mailing list, be sure to alert them to your Fan Page so they can click the link and join! The same goes for your personal Facebook page; invite anyone you're friends with to "Like" your Fan Page and to follow you over there for the latest news and updates.

- Add your Facebook Fan Page link to your email signature.

- Fan other authors and/or books in your topic; authors can and should support each other and this also increases your exposure and allows

people interested in your topic to find you through these other Facebook pages.
- Join groups on Facebook with topics related to your book—another way to network and make contacts.

Update your content regularly

- Your Wall is the most important piece of real estate on your Fan Page. The truth is, busy people may not spend much time visiting the other tabs on your Fan Page, so making the wall lively and interesting is key.
- When you update your wall regularly and frequently, the updates will appear in your fans' newsfeeds—don't just post messages but photos from events, video—anything visual is a big draw!
- Think about making it a two-way conversation: you can hold contests, have a question of the day, host polls, post your reviews and interviews, ask your fans to post some content—ask them to suggest their own strategies for getting outside, green living, healthy tips, etc.
- Run your blog feed through your Facebook Fan Page so you automatically have new content available on your Facebook page whenever you update your blog. Your Twitter feed is now set to automatically send out a Tweet when your Facebook Fan Page is updated.
- You can also post book excerpts, and if you have a topic that's in the news, or find something newsworthy that's writing/book/publishing related, you can post the link to the news item, add your own comments and invite others to join in the conversation.
- The page is quite easy to update—when you're signed in you'll see, on the top left side under the photo, "Edit this page." When you click on each tab, you'll see the "Edit information" logo on the top right. Facebook is pretty streamlined in its setup, so using the Fan Page is relatively easy to learn, especially if you are already on Facebook.

Other ways to connect

You want to get out there and connect on Facebook with potential fans, who can then "Like" your page. Use the Facebook search function to find people or search by keyword terms to find them and invite them to your page.

Don't forget to interact with your friends and fans—that's what social media is all about.

Is it working? The stats tell the story

Don't forget to check your stats; the Insights tool on your page will let you know how many visitors your Fan Page gets, what they liked and so forth. This will give you a good sense of what your fans are interested in, what causes them to Like something on your page or comment. It will look like this:

- +41 Fans this week (3,284 total Fans)
- 31 Wall Posts, Comments, and Likes this week (68 last week)
- 1,477 visits to your page this week (1,869 visits last week)
- And finally... have fun!

Additional resources

http://www.facebook.com/FacebookPages

Contributed by Paula Krapf, COO Author Marketing Experts, Inc.

STRATEGY 26: 10 SECRETS OF A SUPER BLOGGER

No matter how many new web 2.0 properties that pop-up like Twitter and the like, blogging still remains very popular. When I'm teaching a session and ask students in the class how many of them read blogs, often only a few hands go up. Want to know why? Because blogs are so pervasive that we often read them and don't know we're reading them. Most people don't know enough about blogging to know what a blog is so when you see huge numbers of people who read blogs, these are based on site statistics, not reader polls.

Check out some of these stats:
- There are now 70 million blogs
- Approx 120,000 are started each day or 1.4 new blogs every second
- Bloggers post an average of 17 posts per second (or 1.5 million posts per day)

How do these super bloggers get such great traffic to their blogs and moreover, how do they keep their blogs interesting? Here are some tips to not only get you up to speed on blogging, but keep you on track:

1. Blog frequently. You should blog at a minimum of once a week and ideally two to three times a week. Don't forget to spell check your blogs, you don't want to be posting stuff that has typos in it. This will turn off your reader. Your posts don't have to be long. If you only post in 50 word increments that's fine. Don't force yourself to post longer.

2. Don't obsess over stats. Seriously. While it's easy enough to get caught up in the "my blog is more popular than your blog" mantra it's not a good thing to spend your time on, also, stats and subscribers will come

and go. Try to limit yourself to checking stats once a week or once a month if you can hold off that long.

3. Don't obsess over comments (or lack thereof). Some bloggers will get comments right away and some will take a bit longer. Just because people aren't commenting doesn't mean they're not reading. This is one of the biggest complaints I hear from bloggers: no one is commenting. Don't let a blank comment section dissuade you from blogging but when someone has commented be sure to comment back or just thank them for visiting if their entry doesn't warrant a response. Also if the reader has a blog, visit theirs as well and place a comment. They'll appreciate you for it and it's a great way to network!

4. Be patient. Let's face it, blogging takes time. Regardless of how many statistics you see on blogs that get mountains of traffic, none of this happened in a week (or even in a month). The quickest way to talk yourself out of blogging is to be impatient for something to happen. Keep blogging, eventually something will. If you do all the right things eventually traffic and readers will beat a path to your door!

5. Listen. Know what your reader needs and blog on those topics. Knowing what's important to your reader is a big step in creating a powerful blog that will get traffic. Know what's going on in your industry, what you should be talking about. What does your reader need help with? How can your blog become a resource? Who else does your reader need to know in order to be successful? Maybe it's time that you interview other experts on your blog or at the very least, link to them.

6. Write good headlines. People judge a blog by its headline and when you're subscribed to a lot of blog feeds (as I am) you know that readers will pick and choose the blogs they read based on the headlines. Don't make readers guess what your blog is about, be specific and be benefit driven.

7. Be timeless. While many of your posts will relate to topics or news items that are going on *now*, it's also good to write posts that will be evergreen, meaning posts that don't have a short lifespan. For example I have posts dating back to 2006 that still get commented on and passed around because their topic is as relevant today as it was three years ago.

8. Posting tips. I generally try to post by 7 a.m. EST (8 a.m. at the latest). Studies have shown that people have more time to read blogs and emails before 9 a.m. EST so make sure all your posting is done by then.

9. No time for the long-winded. Write readable posts. Keep your sentences to no more than 25 words and paragraphs to no more than seven lines of text. Use bullet points whenever you can.

Get your own domain name early. There's nothing worse than getting a blog that's someone else's property (i.e. Blogger or Wordpress). If you wait too long to move your blog to your own domain you'll risk losing search engine ranking and traffic. Any blog can be linked to any URL, just ask your web person to help you out with this.

So now that you have your tips, what on earth will you blog on? Here are a few ideas to consider:

Trends, write reviews, interview experts, comment on news pieces related to your topic, blog on good reviews your book received, blog on your new book, blog on the elephant in the room (talk about the thing everyone seems to be avoiding).

Happy Blogging!

SOCIAL NETWORKING ON BLOGS

We're all familiar with networking at meetings, right? And we've definitely heard of social networking, but do you know how to network on blogs?

We all know that it's great to hop on social networks like Facebook, Squidoo and Twitter, right? But have you ever considered that a blog is a social network too? You bet it is, but I'm talking specifically about the comment section within each blog. We all know that it's great to pitch bloggers for your book or product, right? But there's more to it. Really, it's about online networking or cyber-schmoozing. Before you even target a blog for your pitch, you should get to know them first.

Here's how:

First, you'll want to get to know the blogs in your market. To do this you'll want to follow them and communicate with them via the comment section on their blogs. You can find these blogs through blog search engines like Google Blog Search and Technorati.com. Once you find the top blogs in your market (I suggest going after the top 5-10 to start with) then you'll want to see what they post and comment on their blog posts. What does this do? Well, it'll help give you a voice on your top blogs and give the bloggers a chance to get to know you.

Here are some tips for commenting intelligently on blogs:

- Be interesting and thought provoking. Save the "wow, great blog" comments for when you are really looking to *not* impress someone.

- Watch, then comment. I recommend following the blog for a few weeks before jumping in. You want to get a sense of the blogger's tone and how he or she responds to comments.

- Try commenting on at least five blogs a week, this way you're not spending *all* of your free time doing this, but still you're able to get a voice out there in the blog-o-sphere.
- Offer additional insight to the blog post, perhaps you've had a different experience than what the blogger cited. If so, politely and intelligently tell them your viewpoint and invite other ideas.
- Be entertaining, engaging, and helpful. Always. Don't push your book, yes you can mention it—but don't push it, that's a big no-no.
- Try to build a rapport with the blogger by being consistent, that's why you don't want to follow too many bloggers. You'll be too fragmented this way.
- Be inspiring, readers love inspiration. Don't just gush for the sake of gushing.

Commenting on blogs posts is a sort of social networking, even better in fact because blog posts and their associated comments are searchable. Keep in mind that you'll want to always list your URL when you log in (and most blogs require that you do log in and leave your online "footprint").

Once you have spent sufficient time online you'll start to get to know the bloggers that are a significant "voice" in your industry. This type of networking will help when you go back to pitch them your story, book or product. Remember that bloggers, like any other on or offline media, want the scoop. So give them what they want.

Here are a few tips for pitching bloggers once you've networked with them:

- Know what they like. Don't pitch them a book review if they don't review books. Just because you have become commenter-extraordinaire doesn't mean that they'll bend the rules for you. Well, they might, but better to let them suggest it.
- If the blogger does review books and/or products check out his or her submission guidelines before sending a pitch.

- If you're sending them a story idea be sure and tell them if you've pitched this idea to anyone else. If they have an exclusive, tell them and give them a (reasonable) deadline for responding if you're going to shop this around.
- Present the unexpected. It's OK to take chances, it really is as long as you stay on topic. Pitch the blogger, you never know what could happen.
- Make it easy. If you're pitching them a story don't just pitch them and expect them to do all the work. Make it easy on them by offering to co-interview (when appropriate) or offering them experts you think might work well for the piece.

The key is that as you're getting known online, the Internet is one big networking party. Just because you can hide behind your monitor doesn't mean that you're invisible. Remember that everything is your resume and everything leaves a footprint. The best thing you can do is get out and cyber-schmooze, the worst thing you can do is be unprepared. Do your homework and remember, online networking (when done effectively) can benefit you enormously both in your online footprint as well as the connections you'll make. Don't worry about spending hours on this, it's really about quality not quantity. Get out there and social network on blogs, you'll be glad you did.

STRATEGY 28
WHAT THE SHOPPING CHANNELS CAN TEACH US ABOUT SELLING

Whether we admit it or not, we've all watched a home shopping channel, even if we just stopped by for a minute or two while channel surfing. Home shopping channels are big and the two of the biggest are HSN and QVC; together they generate a combined total of $10 billion in sales every year. They are geared to selling 24/7. What can we learn from this mode of sales? Well, actually a lot. When you break down their method of selling you'll see quite a bit of brilliance behind the shopping channels' strategy that can be applied to your own marketing and sales efforts.

Details, details: The first thing the host will do is give you an overview and then zero in on the details, pieces, parts and bonuses. When you're showcasing your book or product, it's important to not just focus on the 30,000-foot overview, but the minutia as well. The caveat is: it has to be exciting to your consumer. The idea is to push the product, then entice them with the details. How will you do this? Start with one, big, overarching question or pitch. Let's say you wrote a book on dieting, you might say: "If you're ready to finally lose those extra 30 pounds for good, this is the last diet book you'll ever need to read." Now, that's a pretty big statement, and you'll need to follow it up with some details that help build your case. See what I mean? If the book has recipes, highlight several and talk about them. If the book has some never-before-revealed secrets, highlight those too and make sure your consumer knows the whole package they're getting, not just the idea.

Repetition: If you've ever watched HSN or QVC you know that their specials are repeated over and over and over again. Telling your consumer once won't cut it, but telling them twice generally won't either. You have to tell people again and again and again. Think about it: how many times are you telling folks about your book? How can you adapt this to book marketing? Think about the different ways you reach out to your consumer. How many times are you mentioning your book? If the answer to that is "I don't know," then you might want to rethink your marketing strategy. Now, I'm not saying that every Tweet and Facebook update needs to have your book title it in, but what I am saying is that if you are doing any kind of target marketing, email, or mailing, you need to make sure that you continue to push the message of your book for as long as you are marketing it.

Results: What will this book do for your reader? If it was featured on the Home Shopping Network you can be sure you would know, and it would be explained to you in Technicolor detail. Often, they will demo the product on the air. Why do they do this? Because the before and after is wildly popular with consumers. Now, if you're not on HSN, how will you demo this? For starters, you can get testimonials for your website. Remember: what someone else says about your book, message, or product is 1,000 times more effective than anything you can say. You can also consider a YouTube channel (think of it as your very own HSN) and get video testimonials, or demo the ideas in your book. If you're marketing a product, demo the product on video. Remember we love to know it'll do XYZ for us, but seeing it is 1,000 times more powerful than just hearing it.

How's it selling? It never fails: during the broadcast, the host will always tell you how well the product is selling. In fact, often they will tell you that it's nearly selling out, thereby heightening the urgency to buy. As part of your book marketing have you pushed your updates to your audience? Have you told them how well it's selling? Share stats with them, social proof, and popularity. Remember, people like what other people like. If a lot of other people like your book or product, tell your new consumers. It will help heighten their excitement.

Packaging, bonuses and oh, wait, there's more! The beauty of this last line (as hokey as it might sound) is that it keeps the consumer on edge and ready to dial, but there's more... so the additional bonuses entice them further. When we offered my book, *Red Hot Internet Publicity*, packaged for a limited time with another title (the offer was "Get 2 books for the price of 1") we tripled our sales. Packages and special offers work, though it's generally a good idea to offer them for a limited time. As you'll see from one of the points below, urgency sells.

Pricing: Consumers love a bargain and the Home Shopping Network knows this all too well, so the discounts are crucial if they are trying to sell out a product. If you are trying to push your book, don't get greedy. As I mentioned in the point above, the deeper the discount, the better the response. Be clear on your price point, i.e. what you need to make a profit, then play with the numbers and see what your consumer responds to. Now, you don't have to offer shippable product as a special offer or price enhancement; it can also be electronic which makes it easier and raises your profit margin.

Urgency: Let's face it; while it might seem cheesy, urgency sells. "Only 10 minutes left to buy!" and suddenly the phones light up. During the process of the sale, sale updates, bonuses, discounts, etc. all help to heighten the urgency of the buy including the limited time offer. When you're running a special promotion, the best way to get people to beat a path to your door is to give them a deadline.

Remember the upsell: When you've got someone's attention, why not try and sell them more? If you have a bundled product, or special additions to your product, be sure and mention it. In fact, one of the most effective ways to generate sales is to entice your consumer by offering bonuses. Keep in mind that the bonuses need to have value to the consumer: they must enhance your product, not detract from it. You likely wouldn't offer a copy of a colleague's fiction book if you are selling a book on building your business. You might want to sell something a bit more compatible like a handbook, white paper, or webinar (either pre-recorded or live). Upsells are great when the product pairing is complimentary.

If you're not convinced by these tips, try watching a shopping channel and see if you don't agree. Their methods of selling are so finely tuned, you'll see a real pattern in how they present each and every product. What that says is: if it works, stick with it. Try one or all of the above strategies and see if it doesn't tip the selling scale in your favor.

STRATEGY 29: THE BOOK SIGNING CHECKLIST

Stuff To Do Before Your Book Signing

- See if you can get a copy of the store's media list. More than likely the bookstore will send out press releases but it's important for you to do the same. Not only will you be able to target the same people twice, but the store manager will also know that you are actively involved in promoting your event.

- Send a confirmation of your signing to the bookstore. It will make you look professional and show the store manager that you take your book signings very seriously. A sample of the form I use follows this chapter.

- Start tapping into that media list you've been creating and begin contacting local media to promote your event.

- Post your book signing information on the Author Appearances section of your website. Get invitations made up or make them yourself and send everyone on your contact list an invitation to your signing.

- If you haven't already done so, get those bookmarks and postcards printed up. Don't forget to include the ISBN of your book, include a few review blurbs if you have them. Get the cover of your book enlarged to poster size. Then, get it laminated and mounted. I have three of them printed up. I will usually drop one or two off at the store prior to the event so they can set them out and I'll bring the third one with me that day. Prop a sign up on an easel by the front door where you will be standing and greeting people. If you have the time and the budget, get a set of colorful pens made up with the title of the book and author's name imprinted on it. Then when you sign the book, give the reader the pen. It's another great way to spread the word about your book!

- Get signs made that say: "Book Signing Today" or "Author Appearance;" both of these will help to draw crowds to your table.

Things To Bring To Your Book Signing

- Bookmarks. I try to hand these out like crazy. Sometimes I'll even hand them out with the flyer when people enter the store. I've even autographed one or two when people hesitate to buy a book. More often than not, they return at a later time to buy a copy just because I gave them a bookmark.
- Postcards. Bring postcards with your book cover on them. I always say you can never have too many marketing materials.
- Chocolate. I like to fill an attractive jar with Hershey's kisses or some other small chocolate. Food attracts people and may even keep them lingering a bit longer.
- Guest book. I always have people sign in at the event. If they give you their email address, inquire as to whether you can add them to your mailing list. This is a great way to build a "fan club" and continue spreading the word about your book as well as future releases. If you don't feel comfortable with a guest book, try putting together a free drawing. Tell them they don't have to be present to win. People hate that; I know I do. I mean who wants to stick around a book signing for four hours? Well, okay, except for the author. You should do what you can to keep a log of people that purchased your book. It's a great way to build your mailing list and customer base.
- Make up a small flyer to hand to people who enter the store. They may not even know about your signing but you'll be sure to tell them. Keep in mind that heavy promotion of your book signing does not just benefit you, it also benefits the store and sends a strong message that you know how to move your books.
- Your favorite pen.

During Your Signing

- Don't sit down unless you have to.
- Smile, talk and most of all have fun! This is no time to be shy.

- If no one shows up, remember, that's okay. It has happened to all of us at one time or another.

- Get people to enter your contest or sign your guest book.

- Tell the store manager that you'd like to sign the remaining books before you leave the store and see if they have "Autographed by Author" stickers for them. If they don't, you might want to think about ordering some from the American Booksellers Association (www.bookWeb.org). You can get these and a variety of other book stickers for $5 a roll. These stickers will really help to move your book.

- Don't feel confined to stay just a few hours. Stay as long as there is an interest in the book. Once, I booked a signing for two hours; I ended up staying for five.

What To Do After Your Book Signing

Send a thank you note to the person in charge of coordinating your signing. Don't send an email. Send a handwritten note. It will go a lot further!

A Few Final Notes on Book Signings

Be cautious of pay periods when scheduling a date for your signing. For example, I will always try to schedule mine around the 15th or 30th of the month. I live in a Navy town and since they never fail to get paid on those dates, it really helps to boost my sales. Also, check to see if the store has a newsletter. If it does, offer to write a short article on your book or discussion topic that will draw more attention to your signing. Keep the article interesting and helpful without giving away everything you plan to share with your guests. Or, if your book is fiction, share an interesting excerpt from it. Sometimes bookstore newsletters are printed by their corporate offices but generally they print them in-house and are always in need of "filler" items.

Also, contact your local TV stations and speak to the producer. Call the day before (if your signing is on Sunday call them on Friday) and let him know you've sent a press release regarding your signing (you have, haven't you?). If they need a 60-second filler, you can offer their viewers some helpful tips on XYZ. Or, if your book is fiction, play up the "local author makes big" angle. Local stations love that. Speaking of media, if you can get yourself booked on a radio show the day before or preferably the morning of your signing, you'll really help to boost interest. If you get some on-air time, consider giving away a few of your books during the show. And remember to tie your book and event into something topical and relevant!

Check the book section of your local newspaper. Many times they will announce author events. If they do, you want to make sure yours is included! Be sure to send them a notice of your event at least a month out.

And finally, send a quick confirmation letter when you do get a book signing. It shows your professionalism and lets the store know you're serious about this.

STRATEGY 30: CREATING POWERFUL CONTENT THAT WILL HELP YOU SELL BOOKS

These days it's a must that every marketer create fresh, enticing content. While not everyone uses the term "content," it still comes down to creating words, tweets, blog post, and whatever content you create, it means extra work for you. How can you keep up with your marketing, social media, and your content creation? More importantly, how can you create compelling content that readers will not only want to read, but that will also encourage them to buy your book?

1. For years, I've been creating all sorts of content. Whether it's blog posts, tweets, Facebook updates, white papers, or HuffPo posts, it's all about crafting helpful information people can use and messages that will drive users back to our website. The idea isn't just to push something out there, but to push it out consistently. The best way to generate content is to stay in close touch with your industry. Keep apprised of your marketplace, industry news, changes to your field because all of this can help to spark ideas. If you're scratching your head wondering how to do this, here are some quick tips to help turn you into a content machine. **Networking**: you should be networking with other experts in your market. Getting to know other voices is very important not just for networking, but also for idea generation. Ideas and inspiration come from everywhere; sometimes they come from tweets you've seen, other times they might come from blog posts you subscribe to, or Facebook accounts you are a fan of.

2. **RSS Feeds:** once you identify your network of experts, subscribe to their blogs. I find that staying immersed in your industry will help to percolate ideas.

3. **Tweets:** as I mentioned above, following experts in your market will really help not only for networking, but also as you're building your knowledge base.

4. **Newsletters:** many experts have newsletters. You should be subscribing to all of them. Newsletters are also a great way to gather fresh, new content ideas.

5. **Guest blog posts:** inviting other experts as guest bloggers on your website is a great way to generate content. Not only that, but it's a fantastic way to connect to new people in your industry. Guest blog posts also help to bring in fresh readers, especially when the guest blogger helps promote the blog to his or her community of readers.

6. **Your book:** if you've written non-fiction (and even to some degree with fiction) you should be able to excerpt pieces or portions of it and syndicate it online. In some form or fashion, Red Hot Internet Publicity has been pushed online. Whether it's in blog form, a tweet, syndicated article, or a Facebook update, I have broken this book into a million little pieces all being used as content.

Once you have a good content strategy, now it's time to plan for your content. I recommend that you take time once a week to do this. Sometimes I'll skip a week, but I always make it up. If you're new to this, treat your content strategy like your new workout routine. At first it won't be easy, but you have to keep up a regular pace until it becomes part of your marketing regime.

Keep your content organized by collecting this valuable content in a folder, either electronically or in a paper file. If you're gathering information electronically, I would suggest using something like Evernote (which I love!) or OneNote. Evernote has a great app for both iPhones and Android so if you see something or get content inspiration while you're away from your computer, you can add it to Evernote and it will sync up to your main file. Tres cool... That way you can get to it quickly and easily. Once you have identified various ways to gather content and you've started building this content, you'll start to see your platform really growing. The more you push out there in the way of information, the more will come back to you in the way of readers and buyers.

How does content help you sell books? The more of an authority you are, the more eyes you will get to your message—and the more eyes you get, generally the more buyers you get. Also, I believe that information builds trust and these days, whether you're buying a book or something else, consumers want to buy from people they trust. Building trust is a big piece of what we do, and content creation is a part of this strategy.

STRATEGY 31
NETWORKING

Now that you're published, it's time to get out there and market. While it's tempting to work solely through social networking sites, you do need to leave the house every once in a while and I promise, it will pay off.

Book trade events and conferences provide an excellent opportunity for networking with other authors. They are also great educational venues offering classes and programs, some live, others online. I'm going to share with you book industry specific trade programs, but I encourage you to look at your market and see if there are any events that you can attend specific to your trade or profession.

The largest book-related conference in the United States is called Book Expo America (BEA). The conference has moved around in the past, but for the next several years it will be in New York at the Javits Center. It's an amazing gathering of publishers, authors, and agents. Endless rows of publishers presenting their newest books by their hottest authors. It's quite a show.

Here's a list of the major book fairs supported by the larger U.S. publishers:

- Book Expo America: www.bookexpoamerica.com
- American Library Association Book Fair: www.ala.org
- Christian Booksellers Association Book Fair: www.cbaonline.org
- Romance Writers of America www.rwa.org
- Frankfurt Book Fair: www.frankfurt-book-fair.com (This is the world's largest book fair, held in Frankfurt, Germany, each year.)
- National Association of College Stores Book Fair: www.nacs.org
- Society of Children's Book Writers & Illustrators: www.scbwi.org/

If you're a self-published author, I highly recommend joining IBPA (Independent Publishers and Marketing Association) and attending their annual conference held the same week as BEA. You can find them at: www.pma-online.org.

Also see:
- Editorial Freelance Association: www.the-efa.org/
- Small Publishers Association of North America: www.spannet.org
- Small Press Center: www.smallpress.org

7 Things to do Before, During and Right After a Networking Event

1) Make sure you have enough business cards. I know this sounds sort of like a no-brainer but you'd be amazed how many times folks show up without business cards.

2) Make sure and have a pen with you at all these events. When you talk to someone and get their card, jot a few quick notes on the back so you remember what you talked about. If you don't I can almost guarantee you'll forget by the time you get home.

3) If there is a meal served, be sure to sit with people you don't know and introduce yourself. It's easy to make conversation with people you know, even better to network with people you've never met.

4) Send a quick handwritten note after the event. While it's easy to point and click and send an email, send a handwritten note instead.

5) Facebook friend them. When you get home be sure and send a friend request to your networking buddies.

6) Follow them on Twitter. It's always a good idea to become one of their Twitter tribe if they're on Twitter.

7) If they have a blog, subscribe to their RSS feed so you can keep track of what they're writing about. From time to time be sure and chime in by leaving a comment on their blog!

STRATEGY 32: 5 FUN THINGS YOU CAN DO WITH VIDEO!

You hear it all the time: video sells. But often we find ourselves with a nice little YouTube channel and one video, at a loss for how to create additional content or what might be compelling. If this describes you, or if you haven't even started doing video for the same reason, then let's look at some creative ways to get yourself and your message on video!

Creating professional content:

First off, don't make creating video too complicated. Just about every phone or device has a video camera on it, and while I don't recommend using phones as a long-term video recording device, it's handy to have with you when you're doing videos on the fly. To get started though, get yourself a small video camera. I used to love the Flip cameras until they discontinued making them, but Kodak has some great devices, and if you have an iPad2 and haven't experimented with the video on it yet, you might want to try it, it's really fantastic.

- **Setting:** Experiment with some different settings and lighting. I used to do a lot of videos in my kitchen because the natural lighting was so good there. You can see a few of them here: http://www.youtube.com/bookmarketingame. It's a pretty basic system, but it worked really well. You can, of course, film videos outside too. This works well for most settings. As I said, experiment with different settings until you find one you like.

- **Editing:** You'll need to edit your videos, but trust me on this one, it's not hard at all. I got the Roxio software which includes an editing suite, it's fantastic and I love it. Very easy to edit, add titles, etc. to the video.

- **Length:** I generally recommend no more than 2 minutes for any video unless it's educational. Studies show that interest really starts to drop off once you hit the minute and a half mark, so keep it short and sweet!

- **YouTube Channel:** I highly encourage you to get one channel that's branded to you. Don't just upload your videos to various sites.

Now, let's look at some fun and creative things you can do with video!

Case Studies: This is a fun way to talk your consumer through some of the fantastic stuff you've done. You can do this with the person involved (if the case study is about the individual), or you can just talk through the case study and show examples as warranted.

Behind the scenes: People love behind the scenes. For our upcoming AME retreat we're planning to film portions of our meetings so we can share the "nuts and bolts" of PR with our viewers. If you're doing a lot of research for your book, or going to special places to do research, this is a great opportunity to do behind the scenes video. Or maybe you're working with your cover person on a cover design, try to get this on film too. The "insider" process is often intriguing to consumers.

Training: Training videos are great and often very helpful; in fact, I do a lot of these. It's the majority of videos we film. Training videos can be about anything at all.

Client/Reader responses: Can you get a reader to talk about your book on camera? I always take a camera to an event, it's a great opportunity to capture input and feedback from readers and clients.

Interviews: It's great when you can get an interview with someone in your field, even better if you can capture it on video. If you're going to an event, always take a video camera with you. Often times you can get an interview right there on the spot which will make it easy.

Video doesn't have to be challenging or a burden to create. It can be a quick and simple way to get the word out there about you, your book or product and, it's a great way to drive traffic to your website. We love our YouTube channel, and we know you'll love yours too!

Want to see our channel? http://www.youtube.com/bookmarketingam

STRATEGY 33
ONE MINUTE MARKETING

You say you're too busy to market your book? Well, welcome to the club. Most of the authors I work with or coach work day jobs and try to cram in as much marketing as they can after they come home from an exhausting day at the office. Working this way can be completely overwhelming. It's no wonder most authors only market their books for 90 days. Who could stand to keep up this pace any longer than that? There are so many things authors need to do, most simply don't know where to start.

Enter the one minute marketer. As tempting as it is, we can't do everything. It's just not realistic. Instead, try doing just three things a day. I found that authors are not only more focused this way but tend to be a hundred times more effective. If you're marketing your own book and you're becoming overwhelmed by the magnitude of the work ahead of you, try doing just three things a day. Some of these will only take you a minute and in one week alone you'll have promoted your book in 15 new ways. And remember, your three things don't have to be earth shattering, they can be as simple as sending a thank you note.

Here are a few ideas you can implement today:

1. Call your local library and sign up to do a talk. You won't get paid for this, but they will let you sell your book (for a 10% commission back to the library).

2. Want to drive more attention to your book? How about creating a contest! Contests are great promotional tools. Design one around the topic of your book. For example, I'll be holding a contest soon asking people for the top 10 things NOT to do when marketing your own book. Get the idea?

3. Pitch your story to a local radio and/or TV station.

4. How's your website these days? Remember, it's your 24/7 marketing tool so make sure it's up to date.

5. And while you're updating your website, why not list it on search engines like Google or Alta Vista. Or go over to http://www.addme.com and let them do it for you... for free!

6. Have you thought about submitting an article to a topic-related ezine? Ezine publishers are always looking for content! If you currently subscribe to an email newsletter that you'd like to contribute to, email the editor and ask them what their guidelines are. Or, you can submit your article by registering at the following yahoo group: Publish In Yours (PublishInYours-subscribe@yahoogroups.com).

7. Have you started calling bookstores for signings? Why not start today?

8. Send your thank you notes! Whether it's to a newsperson who did a feature on you or to the bookstore manager who recently hosted your book signing, saying "thank you" is a great marketing tool!

9. Magazine articles are a great way to get exposure. Why not submit an article (or book excerpt) to a topic-related magazine today?

10. Are you a member of all the pertinent organizations in your field of writing? If not, you should be. For example, if you wrote a mystery novel you should think about joining a mystery-writing group in your area. Not only will you be able to promote your book at meetings but also most groups are always looking for speakers.

Happy Marketing!

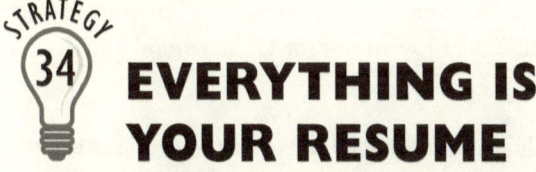

STRATEGY 34
EVERYTHING IS YOUR RESUME

When it comes to book promotion, the title of this strategy is truer now than it ever was. When you put something online, it can almost live forever. That means that we have to be careful what we share, what we say, and the footprints we leave online. A bad first impression is tough to recover from and in some cases it might not just mean a lost sale, but a lost media opportunity.

Here are a few guidelines to consider when forging your success online!

1. **Article Syndication.** Edit, edit, edit. I can't say this enough. We do a lot of article syndication and I can't tell you how much editing we do for some of our authors. But when you're syndicating yourself, who do you turn to? Well, get an editor to do project work for you. I really recommend it. Once an article is "out there" it's almost impossible to get it back.

2. **Blog posts.** Edit, edit, edit. Never put up a single blog post without running spell check (thankfully most blog software comes with this now), but be cautious about this. Remember, it's public domain and blog posts that go up generally stay up unless you pull them down. They'll get spidered, you might even get folks linking to them.

3. **Twitter Tweets.** This is a big one, especially since more of us are hopping on Twitter these days. All of your Tweets can be searched, and it's pretty easy to shoot off a quickie, short, and thoughtless Tweet. Remember that in the case of Twitter, the world is watching. My rule of thumb? Don't Tweet anything you wouldn't want your Grandmother to read.

4. **Facebook updates.** This is another cautionary tale, and not always just

from your updates. As with anything online, be cautious about the type and amount of personal information you give away. Remember, like we've been saying, everything is your resume. If you need a personal page then get one, but keep the business/book stuff to a Fan Page that's isolated to the message. You don't necessarily want all of your readers to know you and the hubby just went out for Chinese food or that you found fleas on Fido.

5. **Online reviews.** While you can't control the content of reviews online, you can control your reaction to them. If you get a bad review, don't attack the reviewer. Listen, I had a bad review on the first edition of *Red Hot Internet Publicity*, and while it was the only negative comment, I wanted so badly to write to the reviewer and begin engaging him in a debate over my book. Instead what I did was write him, first thanking him for the time he took to read the book and then I offered insight on the negative points he mentioned. I also thanked him for his feedback, which, once I stepped back from the harshness of his words, was actually really helpful. Don't battle an online reviewer. You put your book out there and not everyone is going to like it. You have to either accept this or stop promoting it.

6. **Blog comments.** Commenting on other people's blogs is a great idea, but like anything else, be careful about this because like a blog post, comments are searchable.

7. **Podcasts and Blogtalk radio.** There are a lot of opportunities to do radio online these days and while it might not seem as glamorous as, say, NPR, it can get you a lot of traction for your message. Don't underestimate the power of online radio and podcasts, they can have a far reach. Be as prepared as you would be to go on a big show. Some of these podcasts (especially through BlogTalk radio) get thousands upon thousands of listeners.

8. **YouTube.** A colleague of mine was commenting last week on a book/author video that was posted to YouTube. He said that while it was interesting, the author wasn't a great interview and the video was sort of flat. Many authors put up video and forget the worldwide reach that this has. They also forget that if the video can be found, a media person might land on it and if your video is subpar, it might nix any chances

for an interview. Don't just assume because you put it out there that it's good. Yes, the media circulates sketchy, off-color videos but if you look at the number of videos that get loaded onto YouTube, it's really a small slice of the pie.

9. **Hiring someone.** With the proliferation of Internet marketing firms offering Virtual Book Tours you want to proceed with caution. We've been offering Internet tours for a long time and we are extremely careful how we represent our authors online. If you're thinking of hiring a company get a sense of who they've promoted and how they've promoted them. If you hire a company that uses "black hat" marketing techniques, you could get dinged for something that isn't even your fault. Black hat refers to a certain type of Internet marketing that uses faulty link-building and spam techniques to get an author or book exposure. Often the exposure is short-lived and very harmful but black hat techniques can show up *very* successfully early on, that's the way these tricksters are poised. Show early success only to have it drop off. In some cases I've known authors to even get their sites yanked. It's not pretty.

There are numerous "easy" ways to get your name out there and that means you just have to make sure the information you put out there is good, solid, yes edited, and representative of your work. When it comes to marketing online, the Internet is one big networking event. Consider this: would you ever go to a networking event dressed in shorts, flipflops and a tank top? Doubtful. You show up dressed up, business cards in hand ready to rock and roll. The same rules apply online. Everything is your resume. If you make that your motto, the world will beat a path to your virtual door.

STRATEGY 35: 50 THINGS UNDER 50 BUCKS TO PROMOTE YOUR BOOK

These days it seems like everyone's book marketing budget is a little tighter. If you're feeling the pinch, or if you're just looking for some great free stuff to do on your own, here are some tips that could help keep you on track.

1. Buy your domain name as soon as you have a title for your book. You can get domain names for as little as $8.95. Tip: when buying a domain always try to get a .com and stay away from hyphens, i.e. penny-sansevieri.com—surfers rarely remember to insert hyphens.

2. Head on over to Blogger.com or Wordpress.com and start your very own blog (you can add it to your website later).

3. Set up an event at your neighborhood bookstore. Do an event and not a signing, book signings are boring!

4. Write a few articles on your topic and submit them onto the Internet for syndication. You can submit them to sites like ezinearticles.com and articlecity.com.

5. Check out your competition online and see if you can do some networking.

6. Do some radio research and pitch yourself to at least five new stations this week.

7. Ready to get some business cards? Head on over to Vistaprint.com. The cards are free if you let them put their logo on the back. If you don't, they're still really inexpensive.

8. Put together your marketing plan. Seriously, do this. If you don't know where you're going, any destination will do.

9. Plan a contest or giveaway. Contests are a great way to promote your book.

10. Google some topic-related online groups to see if you can network with them.

11. Send thank you notes to people who have been helpful to you.

12. Send your book out to at least 10 book reviewers this week.

13. Do a quick Internet search for local writers' conferences or book festivals you can attend.

14. Create an email signature for every email you send; email signatures are a great way to promote your book and message.

15. Put the contents of your website: book description, bio, Q&A, and interviews on CD to have on hand when the media comes calling!

16. Submit your website to the top five directories: Google, MSN, Alexa, Yahoo, and DMOZ.

17. Write a great press release and submit it to free online press release sites like: www.prlog.org/; www.1888pressrelease.com/; http://i-newswire.com/; www.prfocus.com/

18. Write your bio and have someone who can be objective critique it; you'll need it when you start pitching yourself to the media.

19. Schedule your first book event at a non-traditional location. Get creative!

20. Start your own email newsletter; it's a great way to keep readers, friends and family updated and informed on your success.

21. Start a Twitter account and begin tweeting. If you don't think Twitter is significant, think again; it's been a major part of our marketing strategy for over 4 years now (before anyone even knew what Twitter was).

22. Develop a set of questions or discussion topics that book clubs can use for your book, and post them on your website for handy downloads.

23. Add your book info or URL to your answering machine message.

24. Start a Facebook Fan Page. Fan Pages are much better than groups because they're searchable in Google.

25. See if you can get your friends to host a "book party" in their home. You come in and discuss your book and voila, a captive audience!

26. Find some catalogs you think your book would be perfect for and then submit your packet to them for consideration. If you're unsure of what catalogs might work for you, head on over to www.catalogs.com and peruse their list.

27. Go around to your local retailers and see if they'll carry your book; even if it's on consignment, it might be worth it!

28. Add your book to Google Book Search.

29. Research some authors with similar subjects and then offer to exchange links with them.

30. Start a Squidoo page and make sure it's linked to your Twitter Account, Facebook Fan Page and blog.

31. Make sure your blog is connected to Amazon via their Amazon Connect program (yes, it's free).

32. Ask friends and family to email five people they know and tell them about your book.

33. Leave your business card, bookmark, or book flyer wherever you go.

34. Subscribe to Google Alerts and make sure that you are getting alerts under your name as well as your book title(s), brand, and keywords.

35. Pitch yourself to your local television stations.

36. Pitch yourself to your local print media.

37. Work on the Q&A for your press kit. You'll need it when you start booking media interviews!

38. Pitch Oprah's new station. Go ahead, you know you want to.

39. Is the topic of your book in the news? Check your local paper, and write a letter to the editor to share your expertise (and promote your book!).

40. Stop by your local library and see if you can set up an event. They love local authors.

41. Do you want to get your book into your local library system? Try dropping off a copy to your main library; if they stock it chances are the other branches will too.

42. Go to Chase's Calendar of Events (www.Chases.com.) and find out how to create your own holiday!

43. Going on vacation? Use your away from-home time to schedule a book event or two.

44. If your book is appropriate, go to local schools to see if you can do a reading.

45. Got a book that could be sold in bulk? Start with your local companies first and see if they're interested in buying some promotional copies to give away at company events.

46. Don't forget to add reviews to your website. Remember that what someone else has to say is one thousand times more effective than anything you could say!

47. Trying to meet the press? Search the Net for press clubs in your area, they meet once a month and are a great place to meet the media.

48. Want a celebrity endorsement? Find celebs in your market with an interest in your topic and then go for it. Remember all they can say is no. Check out the Screen Actors Guild for a list of celeb representatives.

49. Ready to get some magazine exposure? Why not pitch some regional and national magazines with your topic or submit a freelance article for reprint consideration?

50. Work on your next book. Sometimes the best way to sell your first book is by promoting your second.

THE IMPORTANCE OF CONSISTENCY

Despite what we may think about the power and flood of information coming at us from a multitude of different places there is still something we all crave: consistency. We want it, need it and value it. That's why no matter what your platform, no matter how you disseminate the information, whether it's through your blog, Twitter, or Facebook, the importance of consistency can't be overstated. Here's the point. OK, so we have tons of stuff coming at us all day long but let's pretend for a minute that at 6 p.m. on the dot, you always turn on the evening news. Then, one day at 6 p.m. you turn on the TV to find that the programming has changed. They're showing an old episode of Frasier. The next day, it's changed again. Confusing, isn't it?

It's really no different when you change your messaging and/or focus in your campaign. Here's a tip: despite how busy we all are we still want consistency. We want to know exactly what we're getting otherwise why waste our time?

Give your readers what they want then give it to them in a consistent fashion. Stay on message, on focus and keep to your topic. In other words if they're expecting the evening news, don't give 'em Frasier. Don't surprise your reader or your reader might surprise you by leaving.

STRATEGY 37: 12 WAYS TO CREATE A MAILING LIST THAT WILL SELL BOOKS

We've all heard this: capture email addresses on your website so you can market to them again. So we do, we capture email addresses and then we wonder what to do with them. What if you don't really have news? Do you mail the list anyway? How can I monetize my list, and how much is too much?

We've had The Book Marketing Expert Newsletter for over eight years now and the newsletter, bursting in content, is one of the best promotional tools my company has. We've never done a single piece of advertisement for my firm, all of it has come from word of mouth, online and our newsletter.

The key to a good newsletter list is simple really, and the biggest piece of this is you've got to have something useful to say. While your friends and family might enjoy hearing about your latest book signing, people who happened onto your site and subscribed to your ezine might become bored with this information and unsubscribe. If you have a list or are considering starting one, consider these tips to get you going and help you maximize your newsletter.

1. **Timing**. How often you send the newsletter will really depend on your crowd, but I don't recommend anything less than once a month. I know some people who send a quarterly newsletter and that's fine if you don't really have much to say, but if you're looking for content so you can send the newsletter more frequently, then read on; I have some ideas and ways of maximizing the use of content for your newsletter.

2. **Distribution**. How will you send your newsletter? If your plan is to email it, forget it unless you have fewer than 100 subscribers. Anything over that and you should consider using a service like Aweber or Constant Contact. These places will handle your subscribes and unsubscribes for

you. If you start mailing to a list larger than 50 from your email service, you run the risk of getting shut down for spam.

3. **Easy Opt In**. Make it easy for people to sign up. Make sure there's a sign-up on your website, preferably the home page and then a mention of it again on your most popular page which, for most of us, is our blog. The opt-in will take new subscribers to your welcome page (which we'll talk about in a minute) and handle sending your new readers right into the mailing list.

4. **Ethical Bribe.** What will you give readers to get their email? It might not be enough just to tout that you have this fabulous newsletter; in fact, often it isn't. Have something that they'll want, a key item: ebook, tip sheet, whatever will entice readers to sign up for your newsletter. Here's a hint: give them something they'll have to keep referring to again and again so that your name and book stays in front of them.

5. **Free**. There are some folks in the industry who try to charge for their newsletters. Listen, I get it. A newsletter is a lot of work, but if done properly, it is a key promotional tool and therefore, should be free. Magazines can charge for subscriptions, you can't. Make it free. Don't even put a value on it. I know folks who do this, too. I think the value of the newsletter should be evident in its content, not in the price you chose to put on it.

6. **Welcome pages**. After someone signs up for your newsletter, what will they see? A simple thank you page on your website is a waste of an opportunity. Make sure there is a welcome page that shares their freebie (the ethical bribe) and tells them about one or two of your products. It's also a great idea to offer a special on this welcome page as a "thank you" for signing up to your mailing list.

7. **Check your facts**. The quickest way to lose subscribers is to publish a newsletter full of factual mistakes. Do your fact and link checking prior to it going out. Seriously. It's important not just to the credibility of your newsletter, but to you as well. I mean, who wants to buy something from someone who can't even be bothered to check their facts? Also, please get your newsletter edited. I've seen some newsletters with a disclaimer that they are unedited. If you aren't an editor and can't afford one, see if you can get it done for free and then blurb the person in your newsletter

as a way to reciprocate. Remember, everything is your resume. Would you send a CV to a potential employer that was full of typos? I didn't think so.

8. **Promote.** This is key because once you decide to do a newsletter you'll want to promote it. You can do so by adding it to your signature line in email ("sign up for my newsletter and get a free . . . "), you should also never go to a book event without a sign-up sheet, and add your newsletter info to the byline of any article you write that gets syndicated online.

9. **Collaborate.** If you're strapped for content and time, why not open up your newsletter to other collaborators? Our newsletter, The Book Marketing Expert, is a collaboration of a lot of voices. We have publishing tips, website tips, social media tips, and the main article. It's a great way to let others have a voice in your newsletter, which helps to promote them—and the best part of this is that if you have a collaborative newsletter you can all promote it to the different people you touch in your travels. This will help increase your sign-ups exponentially because you're hitting that many more people. Your collaborators should be in the industry, but specializing in different areas. This will give your newsletter the flavor and interest it needs. Don't worry about sharing your newsletter space with others, we've done it this way for years, and it's a great way to build lots of useful content.

10. **Be generous.** Give lots of good information. By giving away good information people will want to read it, and when they read it you will build a readership and loyal following, not just for your newsletter but for your books and products as well.

11. **Balance.** The key to a good newsletter that will not only get read, but passed along, is balance. By this I mean balance giving with selling. My general rule of thumb is 95% helpful information and 5% selling; while that number may seem low trust me, this is a great balance. Yes, you can offer specials and offers to your readers, but that's the 5%.

12. **Content creation.** While it may seem daunting to have to write content for a newsletter every month or every two weeks, you can use and reuse this content because not everyone will find you in the same place. What I mean by this is that some folks will find you on your blog, others might find you on Twitter and still others will find you by searching online and

happening on an article you've syndicated. Once I create content for The Book Marketing Expert Newsletter, that content is then redistributed and reused in places like our blog, my Twitter account (@bookgal) our Facebook Fan Page or on my page at The Huffington Post. Use and reuse your content, though not too much. I generally will use my articles in one or two other places and that's it, but the point is that they can be used again.

The idea behind a good newsletter is one that not only brings your readers in, but keeps them interested. It's the marketing funnel we marketing people love to talk about so much, once you get someone to sign up, stay on their radar screen with helpful content. Once you do, you'll find not only loyal readers, but loyal buyers as well.

STRATEGY 38: 30 WAYS TO MAKE YOURSELF IRRESISTIBLE TO THE MEDIA

There is a reason so many pitches get rejected by the media. On average, the media rejects 95% of pitches they get. How can you become part of the 5% that get picked up for a story? First, you need to know the reasons why pitches get rejected. Keep in mind these aren't the only reasons, but certainly the majority of them:

Uninteresting email subject lines: Often your pitch is judged by the subject line. Make it something interesting, make it a headline or risk getting relegated to the delete bin.

Long emails: I don't know about you, but I hate reading long emails. The media hates it even more, in fact many of my media friends have told me that if they have to scroll through a pitch, they often won't consider it unless it comes from a very trusted source. How long is too long? If you can read it on the screen without scrolling down, you're in good shape.

Non-compelling topics: You won't get attention for your topic just because you pitch it. It has to be timely, unique, and relevant to the audience they serve. Think HUH: Hip, Unique, and Helpful.

An opened email isn't always a sure bet: Even if your email gets opened, it might still get deleted, here's why: For all of the above reasons. Create a tight, focused pitch that isn't too long and stays on topic. This will increase your chances that the media will read it through.

Not relevant: What I mean by this is that it's not relevant to the audience the media outlet serves. Don't think for a minute that just because you find it interesting and compelling that your media target will. For example, I once had an author tell me about the amazing world of fly fishing, and then insist that Oprah would be interested in this topic. Really? I think not so much. Watch the show, listen to the broadcast, or read the blog or publication—before pitching.

A false sense of urgency: Often I find that folks pitching, in order to get noticed, will call upon a false sense of urgency. Yes, it's urgent that we fix our school systems. Yes, it's urgent that we clean up the environment. Neither of these things are going to blow up tomorrow so don't pitch them as though they are. While it might make for a more compelling pitch, it will only serve to paint you as an unreliable and often excitable source. Neither of these are good.

Unknown senders: An unknown source or sender may be considered an unreliable one. It's easy enough to get to know the media long before you start pitching. And I highly recommend that you do so.

Now, let's look at 30 things you can do to make yourself, and your pitches, irresistible to the media!

1. Start early and Focus on Relationships.
2. Connect on Twitter, Facebook, and LinkedIn: get to know your media, connect with any local and national reporters, journalists, and news people via these social sites so you can get to know them.
3. Comment on postings via Twitter and Facebook: comment on their postings and news when appropriate.
4. Facebook birthdays: this is a great way to connect to everyone on your list, especially media. Wish them a happy birthday, they'll appreciate it.
5. Watch those Twitter hashtags: as you follow your media, you'll start to see a trend of most-used Twitter hashtags, I highly recommend you follow them so you can see who else is talking about the story.
6. Blog about them on your site, referencing a recent story they did.

7. Comment on their stories, whether it's on their site or on their media site.

8. Sign up for Helpareporter.com (HARO) and respond to stories appropriate to your topic.

9. Get to know your smaller, regional publications, and also trade publications. Both of these tend to be easier to get to and could offer you some exposure well in advance of your book launch.

10. Get to know your local radio hosts, or the hosts of stations you'll be targeting. Especially in radio, it's great to get connected to the broadcast people as early as you can. They also tend to be pretty accessible.

11. Go to events where you know you might meet some media folk. This is often a great way to engage them on mutual ground. Attending the same event is a great way to start a dialog or relationship with the media.

12. Practice your elevator pitch! What's an elevator pitch? It's a short, succinct description of your topic or pitch. Short enough to keep them interested (1-2 sentences) but long enough to tell the story, or at least the headline.

13. Become a source for your target media: becoming a media source is something we'd all love to do. But this takes time. By getting to know your media, commenting on stories they write and letting them know your area of expertise, you might become one of their regular sources!

14. Become a connector: be the person the media goes to for other experts as well. How do you do this? Whenever you introduce yourself to media, make sure they know your area of expertise and your ability to connect them to other experts who might be helpful as well.

15. Every now and then, I will share a blog post with a journalist that I think will be helpful to them. I don't do this a lot—just every once in a while.

16. Be succinct: define your story in one sentence. Keep it short, sweet, and relevant to your topic.

17. Sell the benefits, not the features. The media cares about what consumers care about, and all they want are benefits.

18. Make sure the media person has all the information he or she needs prior to the interview. This is especially true for late/breaking news. If there are new developments, make sure they are aware of them. This will save them research time and make them look good!

19. Speaking of making media look good, this is your job as well. Yes! It's important to make them look good, give them a set of questions, a synopsis about the book or interview topic and be prepared in case they ask you a question that doesn't seem quite right. Sometimes the person who is interviewing you doesn't get the media packet till 10 minutes before they go on, which doesn't leave them a lot of time to prepare. Be sure to help make their job easy!

20. Jump on breaking news when it happens and be ready when the media calls.

21. Be flexible. If a reporter covering a big story wants to chat with you on a weekend or late at night/early morning, say Yes.

22. Be excited about your topic: if you're not excited, how do you expect the media to be?

23. Never, ever give up. It might take a while for you to hear back, and sometimes (most times) the media won't respond to you until they have a need for your story.

24. Keep it short. Write short emails, always. Generally media folk are on email overload anyway; don't add to that with long, elaborate emails.

25. Think locally when appropriate: craft a local spin to a national story. While local media will always cover local, they love regional angles to stories that are making national news.

26. Stay on topic: when you do get the interview, stay on topic. Don't stray all over the place, you will confuse the media person and you'll end up getting a much smaller piece of a story if you look too fragmented.

27. Respond immediately: even if you are on vacation, reply right away to all media queries.

28. Don't tell the media anything you don't want to see in print. Assume everything you say is "on the record" even if you ask them to keep it

confidential. I've seen authors say "well, off the record;" when it comes to media, assume there's no such thing.

29. Avoid slang and industry jargon: it will confuse the media.

30. Be grateful: always. Send a handwritten thank you note after an interview, and even if you didn't get the interview for which you were being considered, send a note of thanks anyway and wish them well on their story.

When it comes to media, get started as early as you can and build those relationships. Remember that while the delete rate of pitches is high, they are still in need of great guests, interviews, and stories. Be all those things and you'll not only be irresistible to the media, but you'll get a lot of placements that could really help launch your career!

Bonus tip! Ready to find media on Twitter? Head on over to Muck Rack: http://muckrack.com/

STRATEGY 39: 4 TIPS ON WHAT NOT TO SAY (OR PITCH OR DO) TO GET YOUR BOOK REVIEWED

If you want guarantees, you won't find them in book reviews. Death and taxes, yes—but the book review process is a sea of unknowns, from how many review requests you'll get to who'll actually post a review to whether they'll even like your book at all.

When you've got people reviewing books mostly as a labor of love, the reality is that review you expected this month may be delayed by a couple of months. Or, they may not love your book and be pretty blunt about it. Life happens. It's fine to check back with a reviewer if you haven't heard anything and had been given a review timeframe. It's fine to correct a factual error in a review, but it's not appropriate to start a fight with someone who has fairly reviewed your book and just decided it didn't work for them.

What else should you keep in mind during the review process?

Be a Pro: It probably seems unnecessary to state that being professional at all times is important, but there have been so many author-initiated blog brouhahas online that we can't take anything for granted. Ask nicely when requesting a review; be gracious if the answer is no. It's not personal. If you've done your homework you may know going in that a particular blogger—who you've identified as a key blogger for your book—is overwhelmed with a review backlog. Perhaps the blogger is up for a guest post, and if you see the blog often includes them, be prepared to pitch some ideas. Maybe it's a good site for contests—again, be ready to suggest a contest and terms. Pay attention to what the blogger does on his or her blog—it's most definitely not all reviews, all the time—and see if there is anything you can contribute to either complement a review or in place of a review.

Be appreciative: I can count on both hands, with fingers left over, the number of authors we've worked with who have bothered to thank reviewers. Do it. The authors who do take the time are usually rewarded by developing relationships with the bloggers they thank. If that blogger enjoyed the author's book they usually ask if they can review the author's next book, and so on. What was originally a one-time situation now becomes an ongoing relationship in which the reviewer follows the author's career and the author has additional opportunities for book reviews, interviews and more—and not only with that blogger; chances are the blogger's peers who like the same kind of books are going to take notice.

Never burn bridges: Even if a review you receive *is* unfair, or not the quality you expected, there is only so much you can do. If there is a factual error, by all means alert the blogger immediately with the correction. Otherwise, if you just don't like the review, let it go. Just remember that whatever the review says, you never know how readers will react and I've seen many cases in which the lukewarm review caused others to say they wanted to read the book for themselves. You're getting free publicity and you have to realize that everyone may take away a different perspective from one review. And you should still thank them, nicely, for taking the time to review your book.

Take the long view: Also understand that the Internet has brought together hundreds of book lovers (aka book bloggers) as never before, and not only do they share their love of books, they also discuss problems, issues and more. Angry authors have gotten plenty of bad coverage this way, with the result being that a multitude of reviewers have sworn they will never review any work by that author. Ever. There's an adage about never getting into a fight with someone who buys ink by the barrel—a reference to newspapers and magazines—but the reality now is you don't want to get into a fight with someone who has a blog with hundreds of (or more) followers, plus Twitter and Facebook accounts and the ability to broadcast bad news far and wide. Don't let that be you!

Contributed by Paula Krapf, COO Author Marketing Experts, Inc.

STRATEGY 40: THE QUICKEST WAY TO KILL YOUR ONLINE SUCCESS

I have a friend who lives in San Diego. She and her boyfriend rented this lovely home outside of the city. They have tons of land, a great house. It was really a fantastic deal. Since they were in such a good place, the rent was cheap and they had no intention of moving anytime soon, they decided to do some minor renovations to the house. This became their "weekend warrior" project. They'd paint, tinker, plant and in the end, they had a great and slightly improved property. Then one day the owner stopped by for a visit. "Bad news," he said, "I need to sell this property and I have a buyer who wants to offer top dollar, in a market like this I'm sure you understand why I need to take it." They had 30 days to move out.

Now, you might think this is a very sad and unfair situation, but it happens all the time. And it doesn't just happen to real estate, it happens online too. It's a great thing, this social networking, but what a lot of people forget is that you don't own the sites you are populating. While Facebook owns the world (pretty much) right now, things could change. But more than that, sometimes a slight "uh-oh" from you and a slight violation of the site's terms of service can cause you a world of grief. We had a client several years ago who built up 5,000 friends on his personal profile. I kept cautioning him about doing promotion on that page as Facebook has rules against doing promotion on a personal profile. He continued to do promotion (though not heavy) and lost his page. He never got it back. His entire tribe of 5,000 people were lost in the minute it took Facebook to pull down that page.

Don't get me wrong, it's great to utilize these tools and promote yourself, but just remember: as much as you might feel "at home" on Facebook, LinkedIn, Google+, YouTube, and Twitter, you don't own these properties. They do. Be smart and make sure you aren't making these sites the center of your success. Here are a few tips to help you own your real estate.

Website: You should always, always, always have a website. I know some authors who use Facebook as their websites. Big mistake. I know other authors who get a website that doesn't belong to them, meaning they are part of a community of free sites they don't own. If the community decides to stop doing websites and goes away, guess what happens? So does your content.

Smart Social Media: One of the things I really recommend is that you center all of your content around your website. That's partially why I suggest linking your blog to Facebook and Twitter. The content starts on your site and gets funneled from there, rather than in reverse.

Other ways to promote: Consider other ways to promote your stuff that isn't social media centric. Interviews on (other) blogs, websites. Yes, you are still putting stuff out there on other sites, I'm not saying not to. I'm saying that you need to make sure that whatever content you put out there is reflected on your site as well.

Duplicate content: There's a problem with posting huge amounts of duplicate content online, but unless you are pushing hundreds of pieces out a month, I doubt you have anything to worry about. However, the flip side is that you want to make sure you have copies of all the content you put out there. If you're uploading a video on YouTube, don't delete it off of your computer because you think it's "safe" on this site. It may very well be, but if you lose your page or YouTube gets bought (again) and morphs into something else, you're in trouble.

Website more: When I talked about having a website, I'm not just talking about having a one or two-pager. I mean have a robust site packed with content. Make sure that you have a blog, and you might consider adding a resource section, etc. All information about your books should be on the site (don't rely on Amazon to house this for you) and be sure that any ordering information is on your site as well. Wait! You might ask, is Amazon in danger of going away? Not likely. But as they've shown in the past by pulling down books and buy buttons without warning: they are Amazon and can do whatever they want.

Traffic: So, the nitty gritty of promotion is what? Sales, right? Sure, and exposure too (though I think you should target exposure first, then sales, but that's another article). If you're sending all of your traffic to social media sites, guess what? Your website traffic is probably pretty low or non-existent. If you send traffic to social media sites guess who benefits? Well, certainly you do in the way of exposure, but long-term this isn't a good plan. Let me explain why. If you aren't promoting your site as the center of the universe, and instead pushing people to social media sites, then your website isn't getting those super valuable incoming links from blogs, websites, etc. that you are promoting yourself to. As a result, your site will sink in Google rankings. That means if you lost one or more of your social media sites, you could certainly pick up the pieces and start sending people to your site, but that will be a long, hard haul. Better to focus on that now and gather that traffic, along with the buzz you create in social media, so you aren't caught with a zero starting point if anything happens.

You might think that the moral of this story is a slightly paranoid "trust no one" mantra but it's not. It's about protecting your stuff and being a smart and savvy author. You would never open up a store in a mall without a lease that locked you in for a certain amount of time, right? While there are no guarantees in anything, you need to be smart about all of these wonderful, free, not-owned-by-you social media sites. You might do a fantastic job of driving traffic, fans, and likes to various pages. But the reality is that you should focus on what you own, your website. I love my social media sites and yes, it's a widely known fact that I'm addicted to Twitter. Yet they aren't the center of my online universe, my website is. Yours should be, too.

STRATEGY 41

5 STEPS FOR CRAFTING THE PERFECT BOOK REVIEW PITCH

Every author wants book reviews—they help build buzz, inform potential readers and buyers about your book, and when done well, give enough information about your book to intrigue without giving away all the pertinent details. Getting ready for the review process does take some pre-planning, as previously covered in 6 Things Your Website Should Tell Book Reviewers About You (and Your Book) and 7 Simple Steps to Getting Your Book Reviewed.

Once you've built a list of reviewers to go after, it's time to start pitching. While this may not be as difficult as achieving world peace, it's amazing how many authors make some big mistakes at this stage, in everything from poorly written subject lines, to impersonal (unimpressive) pitches, to not providing the appropriate book details.

Simplicity rules: Your email subject line should be brief, yet clear. "Review request: (Name of Book/genre)" is quite effective. You don't have room to write a novel on the subject line and you want the recipient to be clear what your email is about. This is helpful particularly if your email lands in the recipient's spam box—a good, concise subject header makes it clear that the email is legitimate. Then, onto the pitch itself.

It's important to realize that thousands of books are published each year so competition for reviews is fierce. The average new book, if it's not heavily promoted by one of the major New York publishing houses, is not likely to get much in the way of reviews from newspapers and magazines. That review space has been shrinking for years anyway. Meanwhile, there has been considerable growth in book blogging and reviewing online; but even with that growth there are still far more books being published than bloggers available to review them. Understand that most reviewers do this as a labor of love and make little to no money. Their review blogs are not full-time endeavors, but something they work into their already busy lives. Learning how to make the best first impression possible when you send that pitch is vital.

Personalize: First of all, most bloggers identify themselves somewhere on their blogs—if they don't sign their posts with their name, the "about me" section typically lists their name or nickname. Use it! When you use a blogger's name one thing is instantly clear: you actually took the time to find out who you're pitching. That's a big plus. Introduce yourself (briefly), and then don't just ask them to review your book, give them a reason—have they reviewed other books similar to yours? Do they specialize in reviewing books in your genre?

If you're comfortable having a little fun with your pitch, by all means do so—I once saw a pitch for a frothy romance that asked potential reviewers if they'd like to sin with a duke. Very catchy and appropriate for the book! But—don't force it—if that's not your personality, then don't worry about it. It's far more important to explain who you are, what your book is about, **WHY** this reviewer should be interested in your book and then provide links to your website so they can follow up, learn more about your book and decide whether they'd like to request a review copy. They will follow up by clicking through on links, so make sure your website has all the necessary information about you and your book.

If you did your homework during your research phase you may know some things about this blogger that might help you get a review request. For instance, if they love a particular author and your book is in a similar vein, that's something you can put in your pitch.

Basics count: Make sure you include all the basic book information in the email:
- Title
- Author
- Genre
- ISBN (the 13 digit ISBN of your preferred format, hardcover or paperback)
- Publication Date (month, year)
- Pages
- Price
- Publisher

And include your website link. (This should also be included on your PR, which you will send out with copies of your book).

Timeframe for replies: You may or may not hear back right away. Each blogger has a different schedule—some people check email daily, others may only check weekly. Be patient. It's fine to follow up in a couple of weeks if you really felt you matched up with a particular blog and didn't hear back. It's possible your original email ended up in a spam folder or was overlooked (the sheer volume of review requests that reviewers receive is pretty staggering). After that, if there's still no word, let it go. Seek reviews from other bloggers. If you do receive a "No thank you," move on, it's not an invitation to try to arm-twist the reviewer into taking on your book.

Additional pitching options: Fiction and nonfiction authors may take a different approach when pitching. For fiction, it may make sense to seek bloggers who review books in your genre; but if your fictional book covers topics that you are an expert in, you may have some other options. For instance, if you heavily researched the history of a city or a historical figure you may find bloggers who are history buffs who might be open to reviewing your book. Sometimes it helps to brainstorm a list of topics from your book, fact or fiction, in order to generate ideas of what type of publications or bloggers or reviewers you should target.

With nonfiction, you're an expert on the topic(s) at hand and should look for your peers in those areas when seeking reviewers. It's much more competitive in this realm, but instead of deciding not to pitch someone who could be a competitor see if there are ways for you to help each other—and use that as part of your pitch. You never know what kind of partnership you can develop if you don't ask. Darren Rowse at ProBlogger covers this really well on his blog, and his blog is worth following.

Two useful articles include:

- How to Pitch Bloggers—Make it a Win/Win/Win Situation www.problogger.net/archives/2010/05/28/how-to-pitch-bloggers-make-it-a-winwinwin-situation/

- How to Pitch to Bloggers—21 Tips www.problogger.net/archives/2007/10/30/how-to-pitch-to-bloggers-21-tips/

- From Journalistics blog—What's the Best Way to Pitch Bloggers? http://blog.journalistics.com/2009/whats_the_best_way_to_pitch_bloggers/

More pitching advice:

- http://badpitch.blogspot.com/2007/09/ready-to-pitch-blog-take-this-quiz.html
- http://www.midwestbookreview.com/bookbiz/advice/rules.htm
- http://www.writing-world.com/promotion/reviews.shtml
- http://www.midwestbookreview.com/bookbiz/advice/fivedead.htm

Additional information

While your PR piece is something you can send out to alert the world to your book and also post to various sites online, it is also a vital document that should be included with every review copy you send out. As a result you'll want to be sure your PR piece—which should be two pages MAXIMUM—has your contact information (phone and email), website URL, book synopsis, brief author bio and the book information you used for your pitch (the listing that includes genre, ISBN, publication date, etc.) You are dealing with very busy people who are deluged with hundreds of books a year and you want to make it as easy as possible for them to write about your book—and what's better than having a PR piece handy with everything they could possibly need—from the book description to the about the author section, website link, book information and so forth? They'll love you for it!

Contributed by Paula Krapf, COO Author Marketing Experts, Inc.

STRATEGY 42: YOUR ROCKIN' RED HOT MEDIA ROOM

Did you know that second only to your blog the media room should be the most updated page on your website? When was the last time you updated your media room? For most of us it's probably been a while. We tend to put up media rooms and then forget about them. But more and more a good, informative media room should be consistently updated. We've found through research, reading, and our own experiences that often it's not just the media that visits this page, that's why the term "media room" is a bit misleading. It's actually a great place to inform, entertain, and educate your reader on you, your books, your message or product, and the things you've been up to and often it's the first place a prospective buyer will go to get more information on you and your work.

In order to compete in the digital age, more and more authors are turning to their media rooms to attract readers to their book. Why? Well it's a great one-stop-shop place to get all the latest data on your books, new editions, new products and new speaking events (should you decide to list them).

The old way of doing media rooms was to have a list of your press releases, maybe a link or two to media and that was that. Now media rooms are almost the nerve center of your entire website. Here's a quick rundown of what should (and shouldn't) be in your media room. Keep in mind that components of a media room will vary depending on your topic, genre and focus so if you can't include all of these that's ok. Better to have only those components related to your book/product/topic than ones that don't make any sense at all:

1. Downloadable picture. Include your book cover or covers, your photo and other related artwork you want to offer.

2. About you. People want to know who you are so tell them! Make sure your bio is on the media room and ready to download. It's especially

helpful if a media person is trying to gather information for an article and wants some background on you.

3. Press releases with live links. Live links in a press release are a great way to get traffic back to your site, but guess what? It works well in reverse too. News posted to your site gets spidered very quickly, so including links and keywords will greatly enhance the visibility of both the media room and your press release. In fact another quick tip is this: instead of placing ads issue a press release. No kidding. Press releases are a far better alternative than an ad on the Internet. You'll get spidered, you'll get ranking and best of all, you'll get traffic.

4. New book/product information. This is the perfect place for sharing past, current, and future information on your book. Be boastful! This is your chance!

5. Tip sheets. We all know that the media loves tip sheets but guess what? Your readers/consumers do too. Fill your pressroom with any that you've created.

6. Where you've been featured. Be very generous with this. Don't assume that if you have only been featured online that you should not list that. List everything! The more you can populate this room with links that make you look like the busy marketing person you are, the more attractive you'll be to your buyer and to the media.

7. Ideas for stories. If a reporter is perusing your site looking for story ideas, why not give it to her? Creating a pop up box that says "Here's how (insert your name) can help you with your story" is a great way to generate ideas for the media and get yourself a mention in an upcoming story or feature.

8. Bragging rights. If you have testimonials or reviews, place them here too. While it's always good to sprinkle testimonials/reviews throughout your site this is another great place to list them. Regardless of whether the visitor to your media room is the media or a reader, people like what other people like!

9. No hunting allowed. Don't make people hunt for information. The other day I was on a site looking for book pricing. I had to send an email

to get a list of pricing, and why? Because it was confidential? Doubtful. But most people don't think to remove the extra steps. Shorten the staircase. Meaning: remove needless steps to the close. Put pricing, information sheets, whatever you have up on your media room so folks don't have to go on a hunting expedition for it.

10. 10) Events. I took events off of my website a long time ago. Why? Because I do so much pop up stuff that I had a hard time keeping up with it. There's nothing worse than an outdated events page but if you can keep yours up, great! Keep it current, the activity will look great on your media room.

A few final tips: don't even consider cramming all of this information onto your site if you're not going to deliver this in pop up form. Check out http://www.amarketingexpert.com/media.htm for an example of this (depending when you click on this you might see different information, our media room is being updated *again* as you read this). Also, deliver your text content in both PDF format as well as in text format so the search engines can spider it.

Don't limit yourself to the items mentioned above, experiment with other media room ideas that might not be listed here. Book videos, for example, might be another great addition to your media room. The key is, start thinking of your media room as a place to present yourself not just to the media, but also to the world! This will change how you view this very important page on your site and help turn a ho-hum page into a rockin' red hot media room!

STRATEGY 43

BEYOND THE BOOKSTORE: HOLDING BOOK EVENTS IN NON-TRADITIONAL VENUES

If you're tired of hearing "no" every time you try and secure a book signing, take heart. Signings have become a lot more challenging since more books than ever are being published each year and stores are cutting back on events. What's an author to do? If you're hungry for an event and not willing to wade through the endless submission process of a bookstore, consider doing events in non-bookstore markets.

What's a non-bookstore event? Well, obviously it's anything outside of a bookstore but more than that, it's a unique location, likely in your city or town. We've done events at video stores, electronics stores, grocery stores, restaurants, coffee shops, even Hallmark stores. When you start to dig into this market, the possibilities are really endless. It's just a matter of finding a place that will make sense to host your event.

Picking the Right Venue

The first piece of this is picking the right venue. The venue can depend on a few things; first, you might look at the topic of your book to help generate some ideas. We once had an author who wrote a book on wine/movie pairings—pairing the right wine with a movie. I placed this author in a Blockbuster Video and the results were tremendous. I had another author with a computer book and I placed him at a computer store on a busy Saturday afternoon. He sold out of some 65 copies of his book in one afternoon. Another great venue is a Hallmark or some other gift shop. Why? Because people are going to a gift shop or Hallmark for one thing: a gift. Autographed books make great gifts.

Selling the Idea to the Venue

This will take a bit of work because it's likely that the venue has never even entertained the idea of doing an event, let alone an author signing. You'll need to make sure they are clear on the WIIFM (what's in it for me): tell them you'll be promoting the event, marketing it to the media (which we'll cover later). Make sure they know that you'll handle the book orders (meaning getting the books to the store) if need be. Yes, there is a lot more legwork involved for these events, but the payoff is huge. You may have to sell the books to them on consignment; what that means is that they take the books and can return to you whatever they don't sell. Encourage the venue, however, to keep a stock in their store after the event in case people come by when you're gone. I've done this before, and nine times out of 10 the books never get returned to the author and are sold instead. Also, in many cases the store will often reorder and before you know it, you're part of their inventory.

The other piece to this is to try, whenever you can, not to go through their corporate offices. Much like doing an event at Starbucks (which I've also done) and Hallmark, a pitch to corporate could take weeks and even months to approve. Most stores have the ability to approve from three to five events per year, meaning that they can have events at their store without having to go through the corporate offices. Most major corporations do this so that the stores can provide community support without getting bogged down in tedious paperwork for event approval. If you can avoid the red tape of a corporate approval, do that whenever you can.

Selling the Books

As I mentioned, you will likely have to do a consignment. The inventory part for most major stores gets tricky, and if the books have to be approved for inventory, you'll end up going through corporate again. More red tape. Try to work with the venue as much as you can so you don't have to create an inventory of your books. The upside, however, is that if the inventory process is easy, you will be on their reorder list for the future!

Marketing the Event

This is the easy part, believe it or not. Local media loves local authors and while that's a good foot in the door—the unique venue location will virtually seal the deal. Market yourself to media well in advance of the event and then again the event day. Also, if you're doing an event in a mall, see if you can get the other stores to participate by doing bookmarks or bag stuffers. Bag stuffers, by the way, are a great way to help the store market your event. You could also do a custom bookmark. With printing so cheap these days, it might be easier to have event-specific bookmarks made up that you can give to the store to help them push the event to their patrons. Make sure you get the store OK first, before you hand them bag stuffers and bookmarks. Also ask if you can create a poster that includes your book cover and the event information. See if you can get a placement on the venue website and perhaps a notification sent to their mailing list. Unlike bookstores that crank out author events all the time, a unique venue that doesn't see author events all that much will be much more receptive to promotional ideas.

More Venue Ideas

Once you take your eye off of the bookstore focus, the opportunities for book events are endless. Consider the following: street fairs, farmers markets, gyms, yoga studios, wineries, art stores, Starbucks, coffee shops, restaurants, grocery stores, airports. Yes, I said airports. I've traveled a great deal and almost every time I go through the San Diego airport, Dallas Fort Worth or San Francisco, I see an author signing his or her books. Look out for this: if you're not paying attention you could miss it while rushing to catch your flight.

Other Benefits to Doing Non-Bookstore Events

The benefits of these types of events are pretty significant, especially if speaking and events are part of your marketing tool kit. Book events held in these exclusive markets will not only take you off the track of competing for space in a bookstore, but because they are unique they will draw much more attention both from the media and readers.

Having a traditional book signing is always great. It will help you get into the bookstore market and might even get your book on their shelf. But if bookstores aren't open to an event, don't let that discourage you from planning one. Being unique will not only help you gain more attention, but it will help to keep you out of the rejection funnel that often comes from competing in a high-traffic market. Also, venue events outside of bookstores are a fun way to build an audience, get your feet wet doing events and speaking and grow your career as an author!

Great Places to List Your Event
(whether it's in person or an online event)

http://www.upcoming.org
http://www.eventful.com

Got an event? Here's how to promote it for free:

Eventful.com will let you post your event and even add photos and a description of yourself, all for free

Craigslist.com—if your event is free you can post it on its community bulletin board, if it's a fee-based event you'll need to place an ad.

STRATEGY 44: 7 SECRETS TO GETTING INTO LIBRARIES

In an economically challenged climate guess what starts to soar? Libraries. The library market is strong and getting stronger. If you haven't made libraries part of your target market you should. And despite all the book buzz online, it's still nice to get your book onto a library shelf. For most of us, this seems like an exclusive right devoted to an exclusive group of best-selling authors. While some piece of this is true, the reality is that if you have a good book, you can get into the library system. Here's how.

First, why would you care about hitting the library market? Because in a slow book sales season, as we've seen in the past few months, libraries are a great way to get to your reader.

1. **What they buy.** Each library gets a budget and it can spend the funds any way it wants. Unlike Barnes and Noble, where book purchases are often dictated by publishers or a sales order from its corporate office, libraries operate independently of each other. Libraries will generally buy hardback and trade books and tend to shy away from mass market paperbacks, but if you're in the latter category, don't let this deter you. There's still a lot of wiggle room when it comes to library orders and a few creative ways to get into the library system.

2. **Getting to know your local library.** If you want to get into your local library it's important to get to know the staff, so dust off your library card, stop by and introduce yourself. Get to know who you're selling to.

3. **Library websites.** If your local library has a website, see if there's a place to make book recommendations. If you have local fans, encourage them to do the same on their library websites.

4. **Library events.** If you've been trying to get into your local bookstore to do an event but haven't gotten much traction, why not consider doing a library event (or two)? It's a great way to get "into" your local library, become acquainted with them, meet your local readers, and well, you know—get more exposure for your book. Many libraries also have reading groups that you might be able to participate in.

5. **Reviews.** Most libraries look to review sources for their selections as well. Consider submitting your book to the following publications for review: Library Journal, Publishers Weekly, Booklist, Kirkus Reviews, and Forecast. These publications are largely ready by libraries and often librarians will buy based on a good review in one of these publications. You don't need to get reviews in all of them (though wouldn't that be great?)—getting a review in one of them should be more than sufficient to catch the eye of a ready-to-buy librarian.

6. **Popularity.** Librarians like to stock what's popular, even locally. So if you're doing a lot of local events, talks, or speaking gigs, make sure and let your local libraries know. Also, if you're going to do TV or radio be sure and alert your library, thus giving it sufficient time to order the book.

7. **Distribution.** It's important to know how libraries get the titles they stock. First, you'll need to get the right distributor for your book. Both Quality Books and Unique Books have programs that can help you access the library market.

    Quality Books Inc. http://www.quality-books.com/

    Unique Books Inc. http://www.uniquebooksinc.com/

    Baker & Taylor: http://www.baker-taylor.com/ (technically it is a wholesaler but can also help you access the library market)

    There's also a nifty little site that will help you locate libraries in your neighborhood and around the world: http://www.libdex.com (libraries worldwide)

Libraries might not seem as "glamorous" as the store window of Barnes and Noble, but libraries have considerably more staying power. Once your book is in the library's system it's in there for as long as your book is in print and the library sees there are readers for it. Also, consider the reorders as your local library will (hopefully) bring in more than one copy. Libraries are a not-to-be-overlooked part of your marketing campaign, and if you missed the review window, don't fret. You might still be able to gain some interest via events and local popularity!

STRATEGY 45
20 WAYS TO DRIVE MORE TRAFFIC TO YOUR WEBSITE AND BLOG

Increasing traffic to your website and/or blog can be a full-time job. But it doesn't have to be. If you understand a few simple principles before implementing Search Engine Marketing (SEM), you'll save time and build a strong and steady stream of traffic to your website.

First, it's important to know how search engines like Google rank you and measure traffic online.

Page Rank: Google Page Rank, or GPR, is a number (between 1-10) that Google assigns to a website to indicate importance. The higher the page rank, the more important the site is. Sites like MSNBC have a high page rank, often nine or 10. Niche sites are lower. Our site is between a 4 and 5. If you're targeting sites for incoming links, make sure their GPR is high enough to matter. Not sure what it should be? Google your keyword and identify sites in your market. The top five to 10 sites will tell you what page rank you should seek.

Google's System: Google ranks websites using two methods: Relevance and authority. Relevance means relevance to the search. Authority is different and critical if you want more traffic for your website.

Authority is how important Google determines your site is and depends not just on the content of your site, but the types of sites that link to you. If your site has 1,000 incoming links from sites with low GPR, you won't get much authority from Google. Conversely, if you want incoming links you should pursue higher targeted sites and get fewer of them. When I started blogging for Huffington Post, which has a GPR of 8, I found that our GPR 4/5 site benefited from the inbound link the column provided.

Since the majority of us search through Google, understanding the intricacies of this massive search engine is vital to getting better results. Let's look at some smart SEO tactics for getting website traffic:

Your website:

1. **Social content.** Have something "social" on your site, whether it's a blog, forum or even social networking. The easiest and best of these is a blog.

2. **Update often.** Always provide fresh content. This helps your rank. What's the best way to add fresh content to your site? A blog is often the quickest means.

3. **Social media tools.** Learn how to effectively use sites like Facebook and Twitter. To expert SEO people, they are considered "feeder sites," meaning they can feed a lot of traffic to your website. My recommendation: use your Fan Page to promote your work and leave the profile for your personal life.

4. **Keywords.** The term "keywords" often conjures up the idea that hours of research are involved to find the perfect keywords for your site. Even if you can only invest an hour, it's well worth it. The quickest way to determine the right keywords for your site is via Google's keyword tool: http://www.googlekeywordtool.com. You'll want to plug in your topic and see how people search on it. The keywords they use are valuable to you.

5. **Ranking for a particular keyword.** Many of us want to rank higher for a particular keyword or phrase. Here's a little-known SEO secret for better ranking: after you determine what keywords you want to rank for, use them in your URL, YouTube channel if you have one, as your Facebook Page name and even for your Twitter account. It's likely the search term you want to rank for won't be available in any of these properties so you'll have to be creative. Here's what we did: Back in August 2010 I had our website redesigned. I wanted to rank for Book Marketing. The results for our site were OK, but often we would show up on Page two of Google. I bought the URL bookmarketingAME.com because bookmarketing.com wasn't available. Why bookmarketingAME.com? Whatever you tack onto the end of your keyword URL doesn't matter and AME are the initials of my company. Using your name or some other branding at the end of the URL is fine, what matters is the

first word or words. When I did that (and I renamed our Facebook Page and YouTube channel too, but not my Twitter account because so many people associate me with @bookgal) I found that within three months, our site went from Page two to Page one of Google, often sitting in the #3 position. Did it help with traffic? You bet it did.

6. **Words on your website.** Once you've identified keywords, use them on your site. Make sure they are on your home page specifically because that's the page Google sees and shows in searches.

7. **Video.** If you're not shy, a great speaker and have an interesting story to tell or great tips for your audience, consider getting a YouTube channel. It's a fantastic way to drive traffic to your site.

8. **Page titles.** Page titles are the words that show up in the top frame of your browser, above the search bar. Most of us forget to give our page titles a name and when Google reads them, it sees things like "home page," which is the least descriptive phrase you can use. Use your keywords in your page titles and be sure to title each page of your site.

9. **Blog commenting.** This is a powerful tool that we've been using for years. Few realize the benefits blog commenting can bring to a site. Identify the top five to 10 blogs in your market and follow them. When there's a post you like or something you want to say, post a comment. When you sign into the blog you should include your URL, this is an incoming link from that blog to your site, which will help you with your ranking, authority, and traffic.

10. **Identify your competition.** If you want incoming links, see who's linking to your competition. How do you search for incoming links? Pop the following into your Google search box: linkdomain:www.website.com.

Blog:

1. **Own your blog.** Whether you have just a blog, or the blog is part of your website, you need to own it. That means your blog is hosted where your site is hosted. Instead of a domain name that reads: www.wordpress.nameofblog.com it says: www.yoursite.com/blog. You should do this because the benefits to your site from an active blog are enormous. If your blog is sitting on a Wordpress site, only Wordpress benefits from

your hard work. You want the ranking and incoming links that a blog can provide.

2. **Blog frequently.** I recommend a minimum of twice weekly. Your blogs don't have to be long; in fact, some of my blogs are no more than 50 words.

3. **Share and share alike.** If you don't have sharing widgets on your site (Upload to Facebook, Tweet This!, etc.) then have your designer add it to the site ASAP. Most blogging software includes these widgets.

4. **Get social.** To generate a lot of traffic we syndicate our blog to sites like Facebook and Twitter. Running feeds is easy. I ran my Twitter feed through SocialOomph.com and then linked it to Facebook. When I blog, it automatically feeds the post through Twitter and then Twitter feeds it to Facebook. Am I worried about too much duplicate content? Not really. I think people enter your message through different doors. The people who find you on Twitter may not be the same people who Like your page on Facebook.

5. **Use Anchor Text.** This is the hyperlinked text that you click on to follow a link. Most people use words like "click here" or other nebulous terms. If used correctly, anchor text can really increase your site traffic. First, anchor text should be descriptive as opposed to "page link" or something general. I recommend that you use your keywords. Where should you use anchor text? Anywhere. You can use it on your blog linking to other content on your site or someone else's. You can use it on other blogs linking to your site (this is preferred).

6. **Write good headlines.** People judge a blog post by its headline, and when you're subscribed to a lot of blog feeds (as I am) you know that readers will pick and choose the blogs they read based on the titles. Don't make readers guess your topic, be specific and be benefit-driven.

7. **Time tip.** I try to post by 7 a.m. EST (8 a.m. at the latest). Studies have shown that people have more time to read blogs and emails before 9 a.m. EST so complete all your posts by then.

8. **Bookmark your posts.** Tag each of your blog posts with your keywords on social networking sites. You must create accounts for each of these

first. Consider: digg.com, del.icio.us, yahoo.com, blinklist.com, spurl.com, reddit.com, furl.com, and stumbledupon.com.

9. **Analyze traffic.** Google Analytics is the easiest to learn, manage and install. Monitor this data a few times a month to see where your traffic is coming from and whether your work to attract people to your site results in unique visitors.

10. **Picture this.** Bring traffic to your blog with photos and images; people searching online for those images may be directed to your site.

STRATEGY 46: 50 THINGS TO TWEET ABOUT

Twitter is a great way to meet people, develop relationships and promote yourself and your book or business. But it's important to avoid being seen as someone who just self-promotes.

Most of your tweets should be about helping others, but you also need to inject some personality, to put the "social" into social networking and help people get to know you. Here are 50 ideas for tweeting or promoting:

1. Teach stuff—teach a little mini-lesson on Twitter. Delve into your area of expertise or just talk about book publishing and how to get published.

2. Share sites or blogs that your followers would be interested in. Be their "filter" to new and exciting information.

3. Use Socialoomph.com to post Tweets to your account for later posting so you don't have to be sitting on top of Twitter every minute of the day.

4. Use Twitter as a news source. You can easily announce news both from your world (as long as it relates to your topic) and from the world of your expertise. For example, I've done tweets on book industry stuff, breaking news, etc.

5. Widen your network—follow other Twitter folk, this will not only give you some ideas for your own Tweets but it's a great way to network with other writers or professionals.

6. Offer advice. Use Tweetdeck.com or Twitter Search (search.twitter.com) to see who's asking for info on your area of expertise and then offer them some help/insight. This is a great way to build relationships.

7. It's ok to market yourself but be careful about pimping your stuff too much.

8. Be original, useful and helpful.

9. If you're on tour with your book or doing an event, Tweet on that and invite your local followers to attend.

10. Tweet any good reviews your book gets, it's always fun to share the good stuff!

11. Every Tweet counts (don't tell people you're washing your cat); don't just Tweet on useless stuff or you'll lose followers.

12. It's not all about you (again, back to the cat) people want to know useful stuff, I know, it's getting repetitive but there's a reason: it's important.

13. Promote your Twitter account in your email signature line and on your blog.

14. Network. Don't expect your followers to grow if you're not following other people. Network, search for others in your area and follow them.

15. Personal is ok. Even though I said not to post useless information it's still not a bad idea to (from time to time) post a personal Tweet or two. Provide value and Twitter followers will beat a path to your door.

16. Follow everyone who follows you. You can use sites like Socialtoo.com and Socialoomph.com to autofollow everyone who follows you. These services can also send a nice welcome message to your new followers.

17. There is a lot of noise on Twitter, and the sooner you get comfortable with that the better. It's like being at one massive cocktail party; you have to find ways to filter out the noise. Sites like SocialOomph can help you do that.

18. Embed a link or some other sign-up in your welcome message; this is another great way to capture emails for your newsletter (assuming you have one).

19. Use sites like SocialOomph or Twitter Search to see who's talking about you and then follow them, too, or comment on their Tweet.

20. It's ok to repeat your Tweets. With the volume of messages people get your followers will often miss some of your posts.

21. Feed your blog through Twitter using Twitterfeed.com.

22. Join Help a Reporter out: @petershankman for Tweets on media leads (it's a great service!).

23. Don't feel like you have to respond to every Tweet, but I generally try to respond to all Tweets that are replies to mine (you can find these under @replies on your Twitter home page).

24. Want to stay on top of your market and find stuff to Tweet about? Then go to Alltop.com and search for your category. There are thousands of them up there. Here are a few to consider: socialmedia.alltop.com, twitter.alltop.com and publishing.alltop.com.

25. Review a product or book on Twitter.

26. Follow big names in your market on Twitter. This will often bring in their followers too, and you want to see what the "big guys" are up to.

27. Get a good picture. Don't leave your avatar blank. Personalize your page if you can, but a good Twitter picture is a must.

28. Tweetbeep.com is a lot like Google Alerts. You can plug in your keywords and you're pinged each time they are used.

29. Are you ready to add pictures to your Tweets? Then head on over to Twitpic.com, this site will let you upload pictures and tweet to them.

30. Use YouTube to share helpful videos you think your followers will love.

31. Music on Twitter is also possible thanks to TwittyTunes (http://www.foxytunes.com/twittytunes/). This site is great for sharing music and it has a simple Firefox add-on that lets you Tweet on music you're currently listening to!

32. Invite people to subscribe to your ezine and offer an incentive.

33. Introduce other authors or experts to each other or to your Twitter followers (they should also be on Twitter).

34. Participate in Follow Fridays #FF and Writer Wednesdays #WW. Recommend your favorite Tweeters by using the #followfriday or #FF hashtag along with their user names.

35. Link to your own articles and blog posts. Shorten the URL using bit.ly so you can track the number of clicks you get.

36. Link to great videos.

37. Ask for advice or ask questions that encourage responses.

38. Comment on someone's interesting Twitter background or clever bio.

39. Offer a free downloadable ebook or sample chapter, with no strings attached.

40. Thank others for mentioning you on Twitter.

41. Link to an interesting Wikipedia entry on your topic or specialty.

42. Link to a transcript from an interesting Twitter chat.

43. Post an inspirational quote or message.

44. Link to other blogs, helpful articles.

45. Reply to someone else's Twitter post.

46. Run a contest.

47. Promote a special offer exclusively to your Twitter tribe.

48. Retweet (RT) someone else's posts, it's a great way to network!

49. Thank someone for RTing your post; it's always great to acknowledge someone for doing that!

50. Talk about the latest trends in your industry.

STRATEGY 47
HOST A VIDEO CONTEST

We all know video is super popular but is there a way you use video to engage your readers? You bet. Besides having one professionally created you could host a contest that encourages readers to create a short video about your book. You'll need to award some great prizes for this; that goes without saying, but think of the fun you could have with a video contest. Especially if your book slants to a younger crowd, a video contest could be a great way to promote your book and get your readers engaged in your message. To see a list of contests on YouTube click the following link: http://youtube.com/contests_main. If you run a contest like this you should look to YouTube to be your primary host. Other video sites that can also be considered:

- www.bliptv.com
- www.eyespot.com
- www.freeiq.com
- www.googlevideo.com
- www.grouper.com
- www.jumpcut.com
- www.ourmedia.com
- www.revver.com
- www.videoegg.com
- www.vimeo.com
- www.vsocial.com
- www.youtube.com

STRATEGY 48
THE POWER AND SEO BEHIND BLOG COMMENTING

For the past five or so years, we've organized teams to support an author's efforts to increase the SEO of his or her website. We've done this a number of ways, but the biggest and most powerful was—and is—blog commenting.

When we first launched teams to offer blog commenting, most people didn't have a clue how powerful this type of marketing was. Most Internet people did and have been doing it ever since. Now it's become more mainstream, and everyone seems to want to jump on the blog commenting bandwagon. But let me caution you, because there's a right way and a very wrong way to do this. I'll explain both.

Creating a Blog Commenting Plan

The first step in blog commenting is creating a plan and, of course, knowing who you'll be engaging with.

Here are a few ways you can get started

Deciding who to follow: Who will become part of your online networking tribe? These are the people influential to your industry. They might be competitors to you, or spokespeople. They might also be authorities in one way or another. Whoever they are and whatever they offer, it should somehow dial into what you are promoting. I recommend that you make a list of the top five to 10 names. Don't go overboard for now. I'm sure there are more people you could engage with but to start, I want you to focus just on a few. You can grow the rest of your list from there.

Once you have your list, you'll want to start following their blogs and also find out where they are appearing. This might mean commenting off of their website, I'll explain in a minute why that's important.

First, let's look at how you can organize this information:
- **RSS feeds:** This is the quickest and simplest way to get started. Subscribe to their RSS feeds and keep all of these in your online reader, or Google iPage. That way you can spend a few minutes in the morning going through your blog posts to see which ones you want to comment on.
- **Twitter:** This is another great way to find content to blog on. Follow your favorites on Twitter and follow the links to their blogs. This will often give you great insights into the biggest and most popular posts on their website. Don't forget to comment on their Twitter posts too!
- **Google Alerts:** Another great system for finding good content to comment on is via Alerts. Plug in the names of the folks you're following. Also, enter their blog URLs too! Often bloggers will reference a blog post and not the name of the person blogging. Having this link as one of your Alerts will allow you to follow each and every mention of this blogger. So, why do you want to blog off their site? Anytime a blogger is featured on a website, it's likely that site is one you'll want to follow too. Or, at some point you may also want to blog comment on that site as well. It's a great way to network with folks who might one day interview you or feature your book!

Tips for a Great SEO Plan

Frequency: I generally recommend you try to comment on 3-5 blogs a week. I also recommend you spend no more than 30 minutes a day ferreting through blogs and posting, anything more becomes a time-drain that will prevent you from keeping up this work.

Engagement: Remember that each comment is no different than a post you would write for your own blog. You'd never consider writing "great post!" on your site and leave it at that, right? You should consider writing short but thoughtful posts for your blog comments. Offer additional insight, another perspective, or a link to where the reader can get more information. Don't be salesy, that's the first way you'll get blasted.

Quality over quantity: As per the above note -- make it count. Don't worry about the number of posts you do, but spend the time considering the quality of the comment itself. You'll find much better engagement and response when you do.

Where's the juice: The SEO juice from this strategy will be apparent in the incoming links that now direct to your site. Each time you post a comment it will ask you for your URL (if you're already registered on a particular site, the login will remember your URL and post it in each comment). While not all blogs allow follow links, there's a lot of debate on no-follow blogs and whether they are still good for SEO. What is "no follow"? No follow is a term used in the SEO world to describe sites that can block your outbound link (the link to your site), using a No Follow Tag. See here for more on no follow: http://www.google.com/support/webmasters/bin/answer.py?hl=en&answer=96569

The No Follow essentially tells Google not to consider your link when ranking for algorithm. Even though you may get referral traffic, Google will act as if you aren't even on the site. Meaning, you may get traffic from the link, but no "link juice" per se. This deters a lot of SEO people, but my take is this: If a link from a high-traffic site will get you traffic, why not post there? We still see a significant amount of traffic from links posted on No Follow sites. Also, keep in mind that search engines pay a lot of attention to social sites like Twitter and Facebook, which are both No Follows.

The point being, a strong SEO plan should include blog commenting. Not just for the SEO benefits, but also for the engagement and connections blog commenting brings with it. Consistent, high quality posts will not only bring you great traffic, but also fantastic connections as well.

STRATEGY 49: 6 SIMPLE WAYS TO PROMOTE YOUR YOUTUBE CHANNEL!

We talked about making interesting and fun YouTube videos in a previous article (http://www.huffingtonpost.com/penny-c-sansevieri/a-quick-and-easy-guide-to_b_926451.html), and now we're going to look at how to promote those videos! First, if you're not on YouTube you should be. Video viewing online grew by 35% this year, which is amazing. Meanwhile there are 35 hours of video uploaded every minute to YouTube, so if you're going to get seen, YouTube is where you want to be.

Make your video searchable: With so many videos getting uploaded to YouTube each day, it's more important than ever to ensure that your audience can find your video on the site. How do you do this? First, make sure you have a compelling title. Use your keywords and make a strong emphasis on the benefits of the video. People don't want to be surprised, and the minute you make them figure out something, you'll lose them to a more focused and succinct video title.

Next is your video description. I see a lot of videos on this site without descriptions and that's a big mistake. Why? Because if you capture your audience with the video title, you really want to keep their attention with a compelling description. Remember, solve their problem, offer solutions, and entertain them. Whatever it is you're doing, tell them clearly in a keyword rich description.

Make them short: Don't push long videos to this site. Short is key, and studies have shown that viewer interest starts to decline as you inch towards that two-minute mark. If you have a long video you want to upload, consider editing it down into shorter segments. Also, while the two-minute mark is key,

I find that education videos can sometimes be longer. We run short seminar excerpts up to seven minutes and they do fine.

Page Layout: When you're setting up your YouTube channel, be sure and use the "Player View." I don't recommend using a grid view which is also an option. Additionally, set your video to play automatically. When you've done that, create playlists of your most popular videos. You're going to keep updating this as viewer preferences change. The dashboard on YouTube gives you a lot of options, use them!

Get a custom channel: Make sure your YouTube channel is branded to you, your book, or your business. A custom channel will help represent your message better and makes your entire video series look more professional.

Annotating your Channel: Have you ever watched a YouTube video and see words or a call to action pop up during the video? These are called Annotations and anyone uploading a video to YouTube can use them, they're fantastic! You can use Annotations to drive people to a sale, get them to another video or video link on your site. Almost whatever you want. If you want to learn how to do Annotations, here's a great article on it: http://www.reelseo.com/youtube-annotations-guide/

Promote your channel: Be sure to push your channel out through social media channels. Promote it on Facebook, Twitter, your own website and even in your signature line. Every time you upload a video you should promote it on these sites, and every once in a while, push a random video to your list to keep reminding them you have a fantastic YouTube channel!

Finally, YouTube got a real boost from Google+. Now you can load a video into the "Hangouts" section of Google+ and watch a video together with others in your Hangout. (Don't know what a Google+ Hangout is? Check out this handy link: http://www.youtube.com/watch?v=Tku1vJeuzH4 It's a great way to share and comment on videos and you should be encouraging your readers to try this. In fact, why not invite your followers to join you in a Google+ Hangout to watch a video and get their instant feedback? You could gather great data!

The importance of YouTube can't be overstated. It's a fantastic platform and, if used properly, can really help ignite interest to your book. Don't burn out on it; getting on YouTube can be fun, lots of fun. But sometimes (like with any social media) if you aren't staying with it, you might burn out or lose interest. Check out my ideas for creating YouTube content to keep your channel going. Be a star on YouTube, you'll be glad you did!

STRATEGY 50
GETTING A HEAD START ON HOLIDAY SALES

You know I used to laugh at the "Christmas in July" ads until I promoted my first Christmas-related book. We actually started the promotion in July and it was the perfect time. Why? Well, maybe no one is buying or thinking about December in July, but the holiday buying season is tough. In order to make any kind of headway you must start early, not just to capture the December sales but also to get in front of any early shoppers. Once those Christmas in July ads start to hit radio and TV, consumers (those who like to shop early) start to gather ideas for their own shopping lists.

When is it too late to start thinking about the holiday market? November is definitely much too late, October is iffy, but if you're staring September in the face and haven't done a lick of marketing towards holiday sales, that might be your last chance. Better to start early—mid to late summer is always great.

Here are some tips to help you get a head start on the holiday buying season.

Events: Start early. If you'd like to do events in December I suggest you start calling stores now. Many stores don't do in-store events after Thanksgiving, but if you have local connections or some independent stores they might be open to this. Speaking at non-bookstore venues falls under the same category: start early.

Promos: Start planning your promos in the Fall. I recommend starting the promo rollout right after Thanksgiving and planning a succession of promotional announcements all the way through late December. If you need to get special pricing on books, or if you're going to bundle your book with some other items, this will give you plenty of time to plan for that.

Website: Now is the time to make sure your website is ready for your holiday marketing. As you begin planning your promos make sure your web designer is ready to go to make any changes your site might need.

Targets: Definitely define your target markets as soon as you can, the earlier the better. If you don't have a good, solid idea of who you're marketing to yet don't use your holiday campaign to test this. Test market early. You'll be glad you did. Don't waste a holiday promo if you don't have to. Knowing who you are going after will save you in costly marketing mistakes (and this goes for any time you are marketing).

Ebooks: I suspect with all the ereaders that have hit the market in the last 12 months—and with both Target and Best Buy carrying ebook readers—you're going to see a lot of promotion for this over the holidays. Make sure your book is keyed into this market, what I mean is: if you had planned to get your book converted to an ebook, now is the time. Also, you might want to offer a special promo, if someone buys your ebook have him or her forward you the receipt for an additional special holiday bonus.

Social media: If you're not on Facebook or Twitter yet, now is the time to join, and even if you are this is a great time to maximize your efforts and plan how you'll use your social media to enhance your holiday promos. Will you offer specials to your social media "tribe" only? Will you have exclusives just for them? Consider early on what your social media strategy will be.

Exposure: Iif your exposure online is minimal, now is the time to ramp it up. Contacting blogs, websites, doing article syndication, participating in blogs, doing guest blogging. . . all of these things are great ways to gain exposure online. Remember, it's not just about the holiday promos, it's about making sure you are searchable online. That way, if someone searches on what you're offering, you'll come up in the search results. This will help you capture holiday shoppers who haven't been exposed to you or your message yet.

The key to successful holiday promotion is planning and enough advanced marketing so that you're not spinning your wheels in the Fall wondering why you're not making any traction. If you're ready to explode your holiday market start early, it's the best way to make sure you have a spot waiting for you when the busiest shopping season of the year comes around again!

STRATEGY 51

6 THINGS YOUR WEBSITE SHOULD TELL BOOK REVIEWERS ABOUT YOU (AND YOUR BOOK)

Getting your book reviewed is not as simple as sending out a pitch; in fact, that pitch is often the first step in the potential reviewer checking *you* out. So we have to ask: are you and your website ready for scrutiny? We've already covered 7 Simple Steps to Getting Your Book Reviewed, blog.marketingtipsforauthors.com/2010/10/7-simple-steps-to-getting-your-book.html. Now, we'll move on to the next phase.

No matter how compelling your book and pitch, those can only take you so far if you haven't taken care of the basics. And nothing is more basic than a website. You should have a website, and your site should be clean, quick to read and simple to navigate. You don't need fancy graphics or inspiring music (in fact, the music or slow to load pages are a huge no-no unless you want people to leave your site immediately). Clean, professional design and easy to find features are all you need.

Your home page should include the following:

- your book cover
- book synopsis
- a buy this book now button
- links to interior pages of your site where visitors can learn more

What your website needs: Those interior web pages should include an author's page with a bio—there should be a short version of around 250 words that can be used with reviews, on press releases and in pitches. If you want to include a longer bio, that's fine, but having the short version ready to use on your site is important. You should have a nice downloadable photo of you that reviewers or media can use. The shot should be in focus (sure, you say 'duh,' but we've seen plenty of author websites with that blurry photo), be professional and not have a lot of clutter in the background. You should also have a quality, downloadable book cover image available.

Include your latest news: You'll want a web page for reviews, blurbs and testimonials, and you should update this page as soon as you have new material. Making this a separate web page on your site makes it really easy and convenient for potential reviewers to check out what others have said.

Excerpts can seal the deal: A book excerpt may not be required, but we highly recommended including an excerpt on your site. Given how competitive the review space is, this is something that can make the difference between a review request and a polite "no thank you." Include the link to the excerpt in your pitch and PR for the book so it's easily accessible.

Make book purchase options clear: Links to buy your book should be included on another page—list all applicable sites where your book is for sale and include a way for visitors to click through and make a purchase. Make it simple to make a sale or you may drive customers away.

Provide contact information: Do not forget to have a page with contact information and include what you think is appropriate. If you are an expert on a timely, in the news topic, or want to make it really easy for the media to find you, include a phone number, as well as your email address. If you're active on social media like Twitter and Facebook include those links too.

Showcase your stuff: Finally, if you've written articles or have a blog, or if you've been interviewed on radio, TV, in print or online, make sure those links are featured on your website, too. Make it as easy as possible for prospective interviewers or reviewers to learn all about you, your book and your expertise.

Bells and whistles won't cover for a weak website—ensuring that the basics are there so visitors can learn all about you and your book (and buy it) is critical. When surfing websites, visitors only spend seconds; if they don't see what they need or want, they move on. Make your site inviting and informative so they'll stick around and hopefully follow up with an enthusiastic "yes" to your review request.

Contributed by Paula Krapf, COO Author Marketing Experts, Inc.

Additional resources

- Your 10 Point Website Check Up
  http://www.amarketingexpert.com/your-10-point-website-check-up/
- 15 key elements all top websites should have
  http://freelancefolder.com/15-top-site-elements/
- Writing an effective cover letter
  http://www.midwestbookreview.com/bookbiz/advice/cvr-ltr.htm
- Writing an effective publicity release
  http://www.midwestbookreview.com/bookbiz/advice/prelease.htm
- How to request review copies
  http://jseliger.com/2010/03/12/how-to-request-review-copies-or-products-if-youre-a-blogger/

STRATEGY 52
10 THINGS YOUR FRIENDS CAN DO TO HELP YOU SELL MORE BOOKS

Successful authors are not loners. They get out and they talk about their book, they engage people, they market and they enlist the help of their team. In this case we're talking about your friends. Getting friends (and family) to help you market your book might be the best thing you can do for your book's success, but how you go about engaging their help is another matter entirely. Friends and family who haven't spent any time in the book industry might be at a loss for what to do and because of that, might end up doing nothing. I find that when I talk to folks they tell me they'd love to help but have no clue where to start. So take this list and pass it out to everyone you know, this should give them a good jump-off point and could certainly help boost your sales!

1. Do you have promotional pieces? T-shirts, postcards, bookmarks, hats, magnets? Send some to all of your friends and ask them to pass them out or leave them in places where your readers might shop.

2. Send friends and family an announcement e-mail and ask if they'll send it to 10 (or more) people they know with their endorsement to buy the book or better yet, if they have a newsletter or mailing list, see if they'll announce your book to their newsletter readers!

3. Have them go into their local bookstore and talk to the manager about inviting you in for a local event or better yet, see if they'll stock your book.

4. Encourage everyone you know to buy a book.

5. Offer them a commission if they sell books on your behalf.

6. If you're in town see if they'll host a book signing at their home to introduce you to their network of friends.

7. Do they have businesses? See if they'll consider selling your book at their offices. (And remember to give them a percentage!)

8. Do they have any connections with local radio, TV or print? Ask them if they'll make a call for you to see about getting you on the air.

9. Tell your friends what you need. Make up a promotional "wish list" for example "I wish I could do an event at XYZ bookstore, or I wish I could get into XYZ magazine." You never know who they might know. Remember the six degrees of separation rule. Often friends want to help but they don't know what you need. Tell them.

10. Thank them for all of their efforts and keep them apprised of your success. Often we get so busy promoting our books that we forget to say thank you and since we hate to boast, we also forget to tell people all the wonderful things that have happened to us and our books. Tell them. They'll be happy for you and it might inspire them to do more!

WHY (SOME) AUTHORS FAIL

Sorry for the buzzkill title of this article, but instead of spreading pixie dust as many marketing articles do, I thought I'd take a hard look at the realities of self-defeating behavior and some of the things authors might buy into that will sabotage their careers. Over the years I've written a lot of articles on how to be successful, but to be successful you must first learn how to fail up, meaning that you learn from what you did wrong, take full responsibility for it and move on. Lessons in publishing are often costly, both in time and dollars. I don't presume to tell you that you should avoid making any mistakes, but many of them are avoidable. Here are a few for you to consider.

Not learning enough about the industry

The first piece of this is simple: get to know the market you are in. This is a bit of a dual message because I'm not just speaking of the market you are promoting to: your area of expertise, but also to the publishing industry at large. Who else is publishing in this area? What are they publishing? Is your area of writing hot or a fading trend? These are all good things to know before you jump headlong into your area. Getting to know your market can help you not only avoid expensive errors but also possibly incorporate trends into your book that could help to leverage its success. How to learn about the industry? Read up on it at sites like Publishersmarketplace.com, subscribe to the free or paid newsletter the site offers. This will give you a good sense of what's selling, who's buying, what's being published. Publishers Weekly is another good resource. If you can't afford a subscription try the online site at publishersweekly.com, or check out your local library to see if it carries any copies. This is a great industry resource.

Not accepting feedback

A couple of weeks ago an author who has sat in on a number of my classes, both online and off, asked me numerous times how she could get onto Huffington Post as a blogger. I told her I would try to pursue a Huffpo blogger for her to get feedback on her work. I did this as a favor because, well, she was relentless in her pursuit of this and I had to admire that. So, I finally got a blogger to review her work and the critique came back not so good. In fact it was terrible. I sat on it for a day, wondering if I should share it with her. I finally decided that if she was so relentless about her career, she would be equally relentless about crafting a perfect message, right? Not so much, actually. When I forwarded her the feedback she shot me off an email saying that many other people loved it and that astrologically this was a terrible time to accept feedback so she would dismiss it. Some moon phase or something. I honestly can't recall. No, I'm not making this up. OK, listen, full confession time here. I have a friend who calls me whenever Mercury is retrograde, "don't buy anything electronic" she says, and I listen. Well, sometimes. Anyway, point being that I get that we're all driven by a different drummer, but if someone takes the time to critique your work why would you not try to learn from that? Look, I know not everyone is going to be spot-on with their feedback, but take from it what you can and move on—better yourself, better your writing.

Feedback is a crucial part to any writer's career. If someone who is more knowledgeable than you about the industry you are in is willing to give you feedback you should listen. Really. In a room of 100 authors I can pick out the successful ones. You know who they are? They are the ones who aren't so wrapped up in their egos that they aren't willing to listen and learn.

Not surrounding yourself with enough professionals

Let's face it, your mother and immediate family will love anything you write. These are not the people who will offer you the kind of guidance that will further your career. Yes, they will (and should) love and support you through this work, but you need professionals you trust by your side giving you advice, wisdom, and direction. You don't need to keep a group of experts on retainer, but you need to know who they are so you can call on them when you need help.

Not doing research

What would you think of a store owner who opened a yogurt shop in downtown San Diego only to find that five other stores were opening within months of his, one of them a very successful franchise with a huge following? Wouldn't this make you sort of wonder why on earth this storeowner would do that, I mean open a store without doing the proper research? Then why on earth would you launch head first into publishing without knowing your market—I mean the publishing market? So many authors learn the ropes after their book is out, and by then it's too late. Well, not too late really because you still have a book, but late in the sense that you can't really do anything about mistakes made and the money it's going to cost you. There are a ton of online resources out there. Get to know them, I've listed a number of them here and there are more, many more. The Internet is abundant with free content. Use it.

Measuring success in book sales

Many of you might be shaking your head wondering how I could possibly say this, but it's true. Book sales, even in the best of economic climates, are sketchy and planning your success or failure around them is a very bad way to market your book. Here's the reality: exposure = awareness = sales. The more exposure you get, the more awareness there is for the book, the more sales you may get. But this equation takes time and in the midst of this marketing many other really great non-book-sale-related things may happen. An example of this is an author who didn't really sell a lot of her books as she was marketing, but found that her speaking gigs started to pick up. Each speaking gig netted her about 50 book sales, and because of the market she was in, many of those book sales turned into individual consulting gigs that brought in much more revenue than a single book sale ever could have. Get the picture?

The other reason I say this is because book sales can be tough to calculate, many reporting agencies don't report sales for three to six months. I know this sounds crazy but it's part of the reason why publishing is such a tricky business. So, if you're doing a huge push in December and you look at your statement in January and find that you've only sold 3 books, it might be because you're looking at sales figures from September or October when you weren't doing any marketing at all.

Still not convinced? Then let me share my own story with you. As of today, *Red Hot Internet Publicity* has been out since July of 2009. I suspect to date it's sold 5,000 or fewer copies. Not impressive, is it? Does that number bother me? Not at all. Want to know why? Because out of the copies sold I have probably brought 20 to 30 new authors on board who will likely be authors for life. Also, I got a teaching gig at NYU because someone handed someone at NYU this book and all of a sudden—there you have it. So if I measured my success by book sales, you bet I'd be depressed. Thank God I don't. Book sales aren't what drive my success. The same should be true for you. Start measuring your success in other ways and book sales will come. I promise.

Seth Godin aka "brilliant marketer" addressed this in a recent blog post too: http://bit.ly/9n1Y9v

Not understanding how New York publishing works

We may not like how the corporate publishing model works, we may find fault with it, but to understand it is to understand how the industry works. For example, knowing the publishing seasons and why Fall is the biggest time for New York publishers to launch a book and perhaps the worst time for you to send your book to market if you've self-published.

Also, know that that corporate publishers don't publish to niches, or rarely do, so if you're publishing to a niche, you may have a real leg up.

As for bookstores, the big six in New York pretty much own most of the shelf space in your local Barnes & Noble, so if you're vying to get in there, you are going to have to do more than show up with a book in hand and a winning smile. You're going to have to promote yourself to that local market and gain enough interest for your book that people start asking for it in bookstores.

Understanding the corporate publishing model means knowing and researching your industry and again, not just the industry you are writing for, but the market of publishing in general. Knowing what's selling, what's not—who's buying, who's closing their doors. Knowledge is power. Arm yourself with it and you'll have a much more successful campaign.

Playing the blame game

If something goes wrong, own it. Unless it's really not your fault, unless you were taken for a ride somehow, swindled or whatever. Own it. Take responsibility. Here's an example. Recently an author came up to me after a class I taught and said she'd pitched 200 bloggers and only 5 of them wanted her book. What was wrong with them? Well, maybe it wasn't the bloggers at all.

Bloggers are busy, busier than they've ever been so your pitch has to be strong and your book exactly right for the blogger you are pitching. If you're not getting a lot of pick up on your pitch you might need a new pitch and/or you might need a new set of bloggers. Don't assume it's someone else's fault. Investigate what happened and take a critical look at the results. If you don't feel you can be objective, hire someone to sift through the data. Assuming success eluded you because of someone else's lack of interest or follow through might be undermining your campaign and you could be missing out on important data that could really help turn your campaign around.

Believing in the unbelievable

There are no guarantees. No one can promise book sales, fame, or the Oprah Winfrey Network. Period. End of story. If someone is promising you these things, run, or if the offer seems too good to be true it likely is. If all else fails ask someone you trust. I get folks asking me all the time about campaigns, programs, and marketing opportunities. Feel free to do the same. Whether you are working with us or not, now or in the future, I will always give you a fair and honest answer. If you'd rather go to someone else, great—but find someone whose opinion you trust and ask before signing on the dotted line.

Success is not about hard work alone, it's also about making smart, savvy choices and not being blinded by your own ambition, creativity, or ego such that it undermines your work. To be successful you need to be relentless, believe in your work and your mission but you also need to be objective, realistic, and humble. That is a successful mix for any author and in the end, isn't really about getting the book out there? Focus on what matters. Good luck!

Helpful Resources

Some great and helpful books:

- Dan Poynter's Self-Publishing Manual, Volume 2: How to Write, Print and Sell Your Own Book (ParaPublishing, 2009) Dan Poynter
- The Complete Guide to Self-Publishing: Everything You Need to Know to Write, Publish, Promote and Sell Your Own Book (Writer's Digest, 2009 or 2010) Marilyn Ross & Sue Collier
- Doing Business by the Book: How to Craft a Crowd-Pleasing Book and Attract More Clients and Speaking Engagements Than You Ever Thought Possible—Sophfronia Scott (Advantage Media Group, 2008)

- 1001 Ways to Market Your Book—John Kremer (Open Horizons, 2009)
- Red Hot Internet Publicity—Penny Sansevieri (Cosimo, 2009)
- Get Published Today—Penny Sansevieri (Wheatmark Publishing, 2011)

Great Publishing Blogs:
- The Self Publishing Review http://www.selfpublishingreview.com/
- POD People http://podpeep.blogspot.com/
- Nathan Bransford http://blog.nathanbransford.com/
- Moby Lives http://mhpbooks.com/mobylives/
- Holt Uncensored http://www.holtuncensored.com/hu/
- The Book Deal http://www.alanrinzler.com/blog/
- Galleycat http://www.mediabistro.com/galleycat/?c=rss

ABOUT PENNY C. SANSEVIERI & AUTHOR MARKETING EXPERTS, INC.

Penny C. Sansevieri, Founder and CEO Author Marketing Experts, Inc., is a best-selling author and internationally recognized book marketing and media relations expert. She is an Adjunct Professor teaching Self-Publishing for NYU.

Her company is one of the leaders in the publishing industry and has developed some of the most innovative Social Media/Internet book marketing campaigns. She is the author of five books, including Red Hot Internet Publicity, which has been called the "leading guide to everything Internet."

AME is the first book marketing and publicity firm to use Internet promotion to its full impact through The Virtual Author Tour™, which strategically harnesses social networking sites, Twitter, blogs, book videos, and relevant sites in order to push an author's message into the online community at sites related to the book's topic and thereby position the author in his or her market. AME has had eleven recent books top bestseller lists, including those of the New York Times, USA Today, and Wall Street Journal.

To learn more about Penny's books or her promotional services, you can visit her web site at www.amarketingexpert.com.

Thank you for reading 52 Ways to Sell More Books!

Ready for more?
Head on over to
www.52waystosellmorebooks.com
for your free downloads.

What will you get?

- Bookstore forms
- Special invites to exclusive webinars
- Updated content

...and much, much more!

Thanks for reading!

www.ingramcontent.com/pod-product-compliance
Lightning Source LLC
Chambersburg PA
CBHW030944180526
45163CB00002B/698